EXTREME ADVENTURES WITH GOD

KAY ARTHUR
JANNA ARNDT

HARVEST HOUSE™ PUBLISHERS

EUGENE, OREGON

All Scripture quotations are taken from the New American Standard Bible ®, © 1960, 1962, 1963, 1968, 1971, 1972, 1973, 1975, 1977, 1995 by The Lockman Foundation. Used by permission. (www.Lockman.org)

DISCOVER 4 YOURSELF is a registered trademark of The Hawkins Children's LLC.

Harvest House Publishers, Inc., is the exclusive licensee of the federally registered trademark DISCOVER 4 YOURSELF.

Cover and interior illustrations © Steve Bjorkman

Cover by Left Coast Design, Portland, Oregon

Discover 4 Yourself® Bible Studies for Kids

EXTREME ADVENTURES WITH GOD

Copyright © 2005 by Precept Ministries International
Published by Harvest House Publishers
Eugene, Oregon 97402
www.harvesthousepublishers.com

ISBN 0-7369-0937-0

Printed in the United States of America

05 06 07 08 09 10 11 / ML-CF / 10 9 8 7 6 5 4 3 2 1

For the seventh grade class at Silverdale Baptist Academy, 2003-04

Trey Abbott	*Timothy Ballard*	*Michael Bautista*	*Brooke Bennett*
Chelsea Benson	*Alexandria Brewster*	*Brandon Cain*	*Rachel Campbell*
Georgiana Carlson	*Hunter Chambers*	*Drew Clements*	*Colby Heath*
Josh Kelley	*Haven Ketron*	*Paul Killen*	*Christopher Kriener*
Jackie Layton	*Jacob Lemons*	*Meagan Lofton*	*Heather McCallie*
Holly McCallie	*Courtney McDonald*	*Tyler Mounce*	*William Park*
Sabrina Patton	*Ashley Reneau*	*Kathleen Shoemaker*	*Cameron Stone*
Bethany Twitty	*Alex Vaughn*	*Josh Waggoner*	*Shae Whitley*
Josh Willmore	*Josh Woods*	*Tori Woodson*	*Bonny Jean Worland*
Lauren Ziemer			

You are so awesome! Thanks for your patience and understanding as I was writing this book. I pray that you will always seek and trust God's choice for your life. Remember, He only wants the very best for you! Keep your eyes on Him and follow His plan even when it is hard and you struggle. Hang on tight to God like Jacob did. Surrender your ways for His. Be strong and courageous!

I love you,

Mrs. Arndt
Ephesians 6:10-13

CONTENTS

Searching for Truth—
A Bible Study *You* Can Do!   6

1. A Struggle for the Birthright   7

2. A Stolen Blessing   45

3. Family Trouble   79

4. Jacob Wrestles with God   117

Puzzle Answers   159

Observation Worksheets
(Genesis 24–36, Acts 3:1–Acts 4:4)   163

SEARCHING FOR TRUTH—
A BIBLE STUDY YOU CAN DO!

Hey! Guess what? Molly, Sam (the great detective beagle), and I are getting outfitted for a great new adventure. By the way, my name is Max, and we want you to join us as we backpack across mountains and through forests, take on white-water rafting, and learn to rock climb as we become outfitted for God's plan. Did you know that God has a plan for each one of our lives and that His choice is always best?

As we begin our new adventure, we will take along our map, the Bible, to learn about three guys in God's plan: Isaac, Esau, and Jacob. WHAT lessons can we learn as we follow these three guys' adventures with God? WHAT will God show us about Jacob and Esau before they are ever born? HOW do these two brothers get along? Are they close, or is there a struggle? WHO is in control? And HOW we can trust God's choice, even when we face struggles and disappointments.

You have so much to discover about Isaac, Esau, and Jacob as you study God's Word, the Bible, the source of all truth, and ask God's Spirit to lead and guide you. You also have this book, which is an inductive Bible study. That word *inductive* means you go straight to the Bible *yourself* to investigate the lives of Isaac, Esau, and Jacob in the Book of Genesis. In inductive Bible study, you discover for yourself what the Bible says and means.

So pack up your gear, and don't forget God's map! Let's get outfitted for the great outdoors and discover what it means to trust God to guide us, even in the most challenging and difficult adventures of our lives.

See you at the river!

GEAR YOU'LL NEED
▼

NEW AMERICAN STANDARD BIBLE
(UPDATED EDITION)—PREFERABLY,
THE NEW INDUCTIVE STUDY BIBLE (NISB)
PEN OR PENCIL
COLORED PENCILS
INDEX CARDS
A DICTIONARY
THIS WORKBOOK

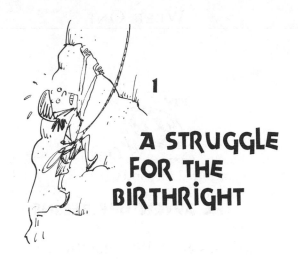

1

A STRUGGLE FOR THE BIRTHRIGHT

GENESIS 24-25

All right—you're here! Are you ready for the adventure of your life? Great! Grab those tent poles. The first thing we need to learn is how to set up our campsite. Then we can get started discovering just who these three guys are in God's plan

Day One

THE ADVENTURE BEGINS

The campsite looks great! Why don't you give Sam a bowl of water? All that running around and yapping makes him thirsty. Now we can go sit by the river with a handful of trail mix and get started discovering the first guy in God's great adventure. WHAT is the first thing we need to do before we get started? Do you remember? *Pray!* Way to go!

Bible study should always begin with prayer. We need God to be our Expert Guide on this great adventure, to lead and direct us by His Holy Spirit. Then we can understand what God says and make sure we handle His Word accurately.

So first things first. Let's pray. Then we will be ready to get started on this great adventure by following one of the guys in God's plan: Isaac.

Isaac's life begins in the Book of Genesis, which is known as the book of beginnings. So let's put ourselves in context by reviewing the Book of Genesis.

WHAT is context? Context is the setting in which something is found. This is very important in Bible study. Context is a combination of two words: *con*, which means "with," and *text*, which means "what is written." When you look for context in the Bible, you begin by looking at the verses and chapters surrounding the passage you are studying. Then you see how it fits into the Book of Genesis, as well as into the whole Bible. Remember, Scripture never contradicts Scripture!

Context also includes:

- The place something happens. (This is **geographical** context, such as knowing where Isaac lived. Did he live in the land of Canaan or in Babylon (present-day Iraq)?
- The time in history an event happens. (This is **historical** context. Did Isaac, Jacob, and Esau live before Noah and the flood or after the flood?)
- The customs of a group of people. (This is **cultural** context. For instance, did Isaac live in a tent or in a house like we do today?)

If you have already studied Genesis Part One, *God's Amazing Creation*, and Genesis Part Two, *Digging Up the Past*, then you have discovered for yourself that Genesis is a book of generations, of beginnings. A generation is what is brought into being. It shows where something or someone came from. A generation shows the order of birth, the family history.

Let's discover the different generations that are found in Genesis by looking up and reading the following passages of Scripture to put ourselves in context as we begin our study of Isaac, Esau, and Jacob.

Genesis 2:4 WHAT is this the account of?

The __*earth*__ and the __*heavens*__

Genesis 5:1 This is the book of the generations of

__*Adam*__.

Genesis 6:9 These are the records of the generations of

__*Noah*__.

Genesis 10:1 These are the records of the generations of

Shem , _Ham_ , and _Japheth_ .

Genesis 11:10 These are the records of the generations of

Shem .

Genesis 11:27 These are the records of the generations of

Terah . _Terah_ became the father of

Abram, Nahor , and _Heran_ .

Genesis 25:12 These are the records of the generations of

Ishmael , _Abraham's_ son by _Hagar_

the Egyptian.

Genesis 25:19 These are the records of the generations of

Isaac , _Abrahams_ son.

Now let's look up one more Scripture verse to find out WHO is Isaac's mother. Look up and read Genesis 21:3.

WHO is Isaac's mother? _Sarah_

All right! Way to go! You have just discovered all the different generations from the beginning of the heaven and the earth. And if you have already done the Bible study of the third part in Genesis (*Abraham—God's Brave Explorer*) then you also know that not only was Isaac the son of Abraham and Sarah, but he was also the child of the promise. All the covenant promises that God made to Abraham and his descendants would come through Isaac.

Now that we have put ourselves in context, let's get started on God's extreme adventure with Isaac. Read Genesis 24 by turning to your Observation Worksheets on page 163. Observation Worksheets are pages that have the Bible text printed out for you to use as you begin your adventure on the lives of Isaac, Esau, and Jacob.

Now read Genesis 24 and mark the following key words. What are *key words?* Key words are words that pop up more than once. They are called key words because they help unlock the meaning of the chapter or book that you are studying and give you clues about what is most important in a passage of Scripture.

- Key words are usually used over and over again.
- Key words are important.
- Key words are used by the writer for a reason.

Once you discover a key word, you need to mark it in a special way using a special color or symbol so that you can immediately spot it in Scripture. Don't forget to mark any pronouns that go with the key words, too! WHAT are pronouns? Check out Max and Molly's map below.

PRONOUNS

Pronouns are words that take the place of nouns. A noun is a person, place, or thing. A pronoun stands in for a noun! Here's an example: "Molly and Max are excited about their new adventure. They can't wait to go white-water rafting!" The word *they* is a pronoun because it takes the place of Molly's and Max's names in the second sentence. It is another word we use to refer to Molly and Max.

Watch for these other pronouns when you are marking people's names:

I	you	he	she
me	yours	him	her
mine	it	his	hers
we	its		
our	them		
they			

Let's get started. Read Genesis 24 and mark the following key words:

God (Lord) (draw a purple triangle and color it yellow)

Isaac (color it blue)

Rebekah (circle it in pink)

bless (blessing, blessed) (put a blue cloud around it and color it pink)

land (double-underline it in green and color it blue)

worshiped (circle it in purple and color it blue)

loved (draw a red heart)

Don't forget to mark anything that tells you WHERE by double-underlining the WHERE in green. And don't forget to mark anything that tells you WHEN by drawing a green clock like this:

That was great work! Now grab those fishing poles with Max and Molly and try to catch a "big one" for your first out-door dinner.

But before you catch dinner, you need to catch your first memory verse. In order to be outfitted for God's plan, we need to know His Word and have it hidden in our hearts.

Look at all the fish that are swimming in the river on the next page. Each one has a number on it. Catch each fish and place the word that is written in its air bubble on the blank with the number of that fish written underneath.

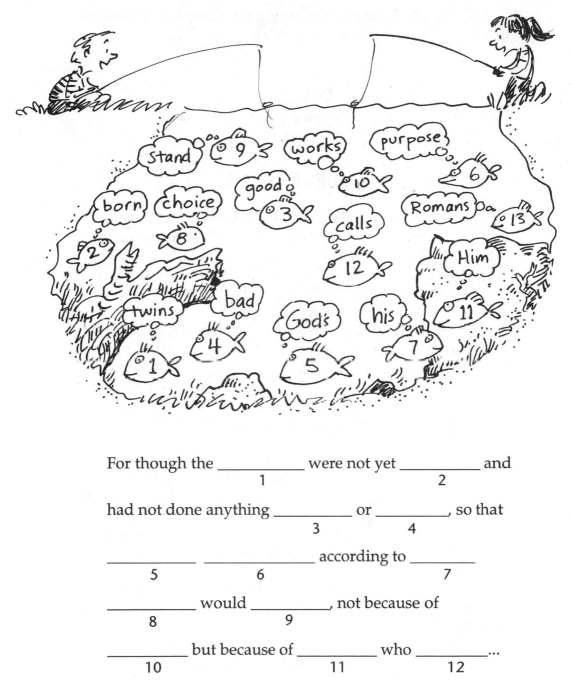

For though the _____ were not yet _____ and
                    1   2

had not done anything _____ or _____, so that
                              3   4

_____ _____ according to _____
       5   6   7

_____ would _____, not because of
       8   9

_____ but because of _____ who _____...
     10   11   12

                                        —_____ 9:11
                                              13

Great catch! Now practice saying this verse aloud three times in a row three times every day.

Day Two

GUIDED BY GOD

Good morning! How did you sleep last night? It's time to go meet our guides and find out what will be our first adventure today. Are you ready? Great! Then race Max and Molly to the outpost.

"Hey, no fair, Max," Molly huffed as she caught up with Max at the outpost. "You took a shortcut!"

"Sure did! You didn't say we had to stay on the path. You just said, 'Let's race.' I beat you fair and square, didn't I, Dad?" Max replied.

"Okay, you guys," Max's dad laughed. "You're both here. That's all that matters. Let's go inside and meet up with our group. Here comes our guide now."

"Hey, guys," Mr. Burt called out as he approached Max, Molly, Sam, and Max's dad, Luke. "Are you ready for your first outdoor adventure? How would you like to get started today with some white-water rafting?"

"Yeah!" Max and Molly answered excitedly, while Sam started yapping and wagging his tail.

"Great!" answered Mr. Burt. "Let's go get you outfitted. You'll need paddles, helmets, sunscreen, and PFDs."

"What are PFDs?" Molly asked.

"Personal flotation devices. That's what we call life jackets," Mr. Burt answered Molly. "After we get you set up, we'll go meet the other kids on your team. Then we'll talk about safety on the river and get started learning how to paddle."

After Mr. Burt outfitted them, he took them out to the river to introduce them to the rest of their team. "This is Alex, Lauren, Mr. Paul, who is Alex and Lauren's dad, and your other guide for the week, Georgiana. Guys, this is Max, his cousin Molly, and Max's dad, Mr. Luke."

"Hey, guys, it's nice to meet you," Georgiana called out. "Mr. Burt always introduces me as Georgiana, but you can call me George. Now come on over and let's talk about safety on the river and how to pack our raft.

Then we need to learn how to use our paddles. Before we can get on the river, we need to be sure everyone is equipped for their adventure."

Good work. It looks like the raft is packed, and you're ready to go. So grab those maps and let's head back to Genesis 24 on page 163 to find out what is happening with Isaac. Read Genesis 24.

Now let's outfit ourselves. WHAT can we learn from Genesis 24 about Isaac by asking the 5 W's and an H questions? What are the 5 W's and an H? They are the WHO, WHAT, WHERE, WHEN, WHY, and HOW questions.

1. Asking WHO helps you find out:

   WHO wrote this?

   WHOM are we reading about?

   To WHOM was it written?

   WHO said this or did that?

2. WHAT helps you understand:

   WHAT is the author talking about?

   WHAT are the main things that happen?

3. WHERE helps you learn:

   WHERE did something happen?

   WHERE did they go?

   WHERE was this said?

   When we discover a WHERE, we double-underline the WHERE in green.

4. WHEN tells us about time. We mark it with a green clock like this: 🕐

   WHEN tells us:

   WHEN did this event happen or WHEN will it happen?

   WHEN did the main characters do something? It helps us to follow the order of events.

5. WHY asks questions like:
   WHY did he say that?
   WHY did this happen?
   WHY did they go there?

6. HOW lets you figure out things like:
   HOW is something to be done?
   HOW did people know something had happened?

Now ask the 5 W's and an H.

Genesis 24:1 WHAT do we discover about Abraham?

_____

Genesis 24:2-4 WHAT does Abraham ask his servant to do?

_____

Genesis 24:4 WHERE is Isaac's wife to come from?

_____

Genesis 24:7 WHO will go before the servant?

_____

Genesis 24:8 WHAT is the only reason Abraham gives for his servant *not* to bring a wife from Abraham's relatives?

_____

Genesis 24:11-14 WHAT do we see the servant doing in these verses?

_____

Genesis 24:15 WHO comes out before the servant finishes speaking to the Lord?

_____

Genesis 24:16 HOW is she described?

_____

Genesis 24:17-20 WHAT does Rebekah do for the servant?

_____

Genesis 24:22 WHAT did the servant give Rebekah?

_____

Genesis 24:24 WHO is Rebekah?

The daughter of _____, who is the son of

_____, whom she bore to _____

Is Rebekah related to Abraham? ____ Yes ____ No

If you aren't sure, look back at the generations we did on Genesis 11:27 on page 10.

WHO are Abraham's brothers? _____ and

_____

This shows us that Rebekah is from Abraham's family. She is Abraham's brother's (Nahor's) granddaughter.

Genesis 24:26 WHAT does the servant do?

_____

Genesis 24:27 WHAT was the servant doing as he worshiped God?

_____

Wow! He blessed God. Isn't that awesome? Look back at Genesis 24:12. Did you notice how the servant prayed to God and asked God to guide him to Abraham's relatives, and to show him specifically who the girl is that Isaac is to marry?

Now look at Genesis 24:27. The servant is worshiping and thanking God for answering his prayer by guiding him to the house of his master's brothers.

HOW about you? Do you pray and ask God to guide you each day, to help you know what He wants you to do and how He wants you to live? Or do you just do what you want to do, instead of asking God for guidance and direction?

Write out what you do on the line below.

_____

Write out one of your experiences of asking God for His help.

_____

_____

_____

Do you remember to bless and thank God for His answers?

_____ Always   _____ Most of the time

_____ Sometimes   _____ Never

Abraham's servant's prayer shows us not only that he knew God as Lord, but also that he trusted God completely.

Do you trust God with all the details in your life, or do you think that you know what is best for you?

Write out what you do on the line below.

_____

Will you surrender your plans and allow God to have

complete control over your life? _____

Genesis 24:28 WHAT did Rebekah do?

_____

Genesis 24:29 WHO was Rebekah's brother?

_____

Genesis 24:31-32 HOW did he treat the servant?

_____

_____

Genesis 24:33-49 WHAT does the servant do before he eats?

_____

Genesis 24:49 Does the servant ask permission to take

Rebekah? _____

Genesis 24:51 HOW does Rebekah's family respond?

_____

Genesis 24:58 HOW did Rebekah respond to leaving

with the servant immediately?_____

Genesis 24:60 WHAT did they do to Rebekah as she prepared to leave?

_____

Genesis 24:62 WHERE was Isaac living? _____

Genesis 24:67 WHAT did Isaac do?

_____

Now turn to Genesis 25 on page 168. Read Genesis 25:20 for
a sneak peek to find out HOW old Isaac is.

HOW old was Isaac when he married Rebekah?

_____ years old

Wow! Just look at all you discovered today. You know how
Isaac married his wife, Rebekah. Isaac didn't go looking for
the right person. Instead, we see how God guided Abraham's
servant to Rebekah and worked out all the details of providing
a wife for Isaac. Isn't that amazing!

Isaac waited on God. He was 40 years old when God provided his wife. Isaac loved Rebekah, and she was a comfort to
him after his mother's death. God always has the best plans
for us. We need to trust Him completely with our lives.
Remember this when it comes time for you to get married. We
need to be like Abraham's servant who sought God's will in
prayer. We need to ask God to guide and direct us in everything we do each and every day.

Now that you have discovered that God is your Guide,
practice saying your memory verse. Then head out into the
open water for a thrilling ride into the white-water rapids.

Day Three

RiDiNG THE RAPiDS—RUN TO GOD!

Look at you! You are soaking wet! That was quite a ride down those white-water rapids. Are you learning how to read the river? Today as we head back on the river, we will have an even wilder ride. We will encounter cascading waterfalls and gigantic boulders as we move from a Class II course with waves up to a foot high to Class III rapids with waves up to three feet high.

Are you ready to take the plunge? Then pack your lunch in your river bag, and let's head back to Genesis. Turn to your Observation Worksheets on page 168.

We are going to skip the first part of Genesis 25, which focuses on Abraham, since this adventure begins with Isaac. Let's start reading at Genesis 25:19-34. Mark the following key words and key phrase:

These are the records of the generations of (circle it in blue)

Lord (draw a purple triangle and color it yellow)

Esau and Edom (color it red)

Jacob (circle it in blue)

prayer (inquire) (draw a purple ⟨⟩ and color it pink)

birthright (box it in orange and color it green)

nations (underline it in brown and color it green)

And don't forget to mark anything that tells you WHEN by drawing a green clock like this: 🕐

Now let's get the facts.

Genesis 25:21 WHAT did Isaac do?

_____

WHY did Isaac pray to the Lord?

_____

Do you know what it means to be barren? *Barren* means to not have any children. Do you remember WHO was barren in *Abraham—God's Brave Explorer?* That's right. It was Sarah, Isaac's mother.

Genesis 25:21 WHAT happened when Isaac prayed?

_____

Genesis 25:22 WHAT did Rebekah inquire of the Lord?

_____

Genesis 25:23 Did God answer Rebekah? _____

Did you notice that Isaac went straight to the Lord with the problem of Rebekah not having children and asked for children on Rebekah's behalf?

WHAT did Rebekah do when the children were struggling inside her? That's right. She went straight to God and asked Him what was going on.

Do you remember Abraham's servant in Genesis 24, how he asked the Lord to make his mission a success in finding a wife for Isaac? And do you remember how he blessed and worshiped God for His answer?

HOW about you? WHAT do you do when you have a problem? Do you go straight to God and give it to Him? Or do you try to handle the problem by yourself or by asking your friends for their help?

Write out what you do on the line below.

_____

WHAT should you do when you are in trouble, confused, or hurting?

_____

The next time you a have a problem or need an answer, remember the examples of Rebekah, Isaac, and Abraham's servant. Pray and ask God what you should do. Turn your problems and hurt over to Him. He wants you to trust and depend on Him.

Look up and read Philippians 4:19.

WHAT is God's promise in this verse?

_____

We are to put our trust in God and not in ourselves or our friends. God will take care of all our needs.

Look up and read 1 John 5:14-15.

1 John 5:14 WHAT is the confidence we have before God?

_____

_____

1 John 5:15 Will God give us our requests?_____

Yes! God loves us. He hears and answers our prayers. We are to run to Him with all our problems and cares!

"Casting all your anxiety on Him, because He cares for you" (1 Peter 5:7).

Way to go! Tomorrow we will find out more about these two children of Isaac and Rebekah. Don't forget to practice saying your memory verse!

Day Four

DOUBLE TROUBLE

"Wow! Did you see that? I almost fell out," exclaimed Max. "That was a really big one!"

"You better hang on, buddy," Max's dad called back. "George said there's another one up ahead, and they don't call it the 'Double Trouble' for nothing."

"Bring it on," laughed Max as they headed toward Double Trouble. "This is so awesome! Are you having fun, Molly?"

"Eieeee," Molly screamed. "I hope I don't fall out! Did you see how high I bounced up that time?"

Mr. Burt laughed. "Is anyone hungry? There's a stretch of quiet water coming up with an area where we can get out of the river and have a picnic lunch."

"I'm starving," yelled Alex.

"Me, too," yelled Molly, Max, and Lauren in unison.

"Hang on tight," Mr. Burt replied. "We'll be there before you know it."

Whew, that was some big water. How are you holding up? Now that we have conquered Double Trouble, let's help Mr. Burt and George get our picnic set up. Then we need to pull out our maps and find out more about Isaac and Rebekah's children.

Let's head back to page 170 and read Genesis 25:19-34. Now ask the 5 W's and an H.

Genesis 25:23 WHAT does the Lord tell Rebekah is in her womb?

"_____ _____

are in your womb."

WHAT is their relationship to each other? WHAT does it say about one people?

_____

WHO will serve WHOM?

_____

Genesis 25:24 WHAT did Rebekah have in her womb?

_____

Now let's make a list to see what we can discover about these two twin brothers.

Esau	Jacob
Genesis 25:25 born _____ r __ __ all over like a _____ garment	Genesis 25:26 born _____ with his hand _____ on to Esau's _____
Genesis 25:23 prophesied by God to _____ the younger	Genesis 25:23 prophesied by God to be s __ __ __ __ __ __ r
Genesis 25:27 became a skillful _____ , a man of the _____	Genesis 25:27 a _____ man living in _____
Genesis 25:28 _____ loved him	Genesis 25:28 _____ loved him
Genesis 25:30 called _____	Genesis 25:31 wanted Esau to sell him his _____
Genesis 25:31 the b __ __ __ __ __ __ __ t belonged to him	Genesis 25:33-34 bought the b __ __ __ __ __ __ __ __ t with _____ and _____ _____
Genesis 25:33 sold his _____.	
Genesis 25:34 Esau _____ his birthright	Nation of _____ (elIsar)
Nation of _____ (dEmo)	

Since we know these two boys represent two different nations, unscramble the words in the parentheses at the bottom of the chart on page 28 to show the two nations of Jacob and Esau.

Take a look at the map below to find out WHERE the nation of Edom is located, and then circle it in green. Next find the modern country WHERE Edom is located today and circle this name in green also.

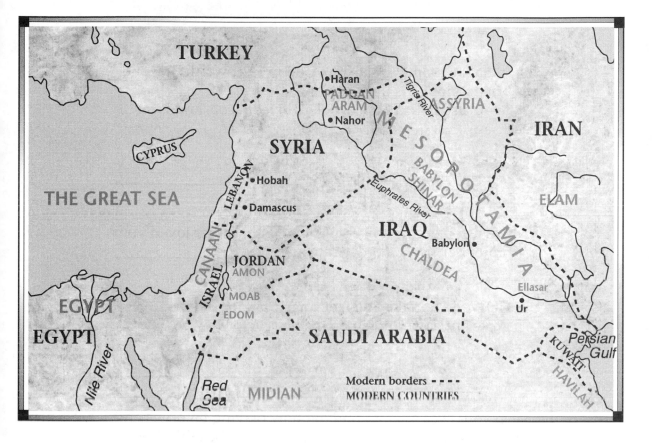

Way to go! We will learn more about Edom and Esau, and Jacob and the nation of Israel as we continue our great adventure.

Now look at Genesis 25:26. HOW old was Isaac when his

twin sons were born? _____ years old

If Isaac was 40 years old when he married Rebekah,
HOW long did he wait for God to give him his sons?

_____ years

Isn't that awesome to see how God in His own timing and
ways brings about His perfect plan?
Did you also notice how Rebekah loved Jacob, and Isaac
loved Esau?

Is it right to have favorites? _____

Have you ever felt like your mother or father loved your
brother or sister more than you? _____

HOW did it make you feel: angry, sad, or jealous?
Write out how you felt on the lines below.

_____

Keep your eyes open to find out how playing favorites and
lying cause some big problems in Isaac and Rebekah's lives.
Now before we head out, let's write the names of Isaac's
wife, Rebekah, and his twin sons, Jacob and Esau, on the
family tree below.

Isaac's Family Tree

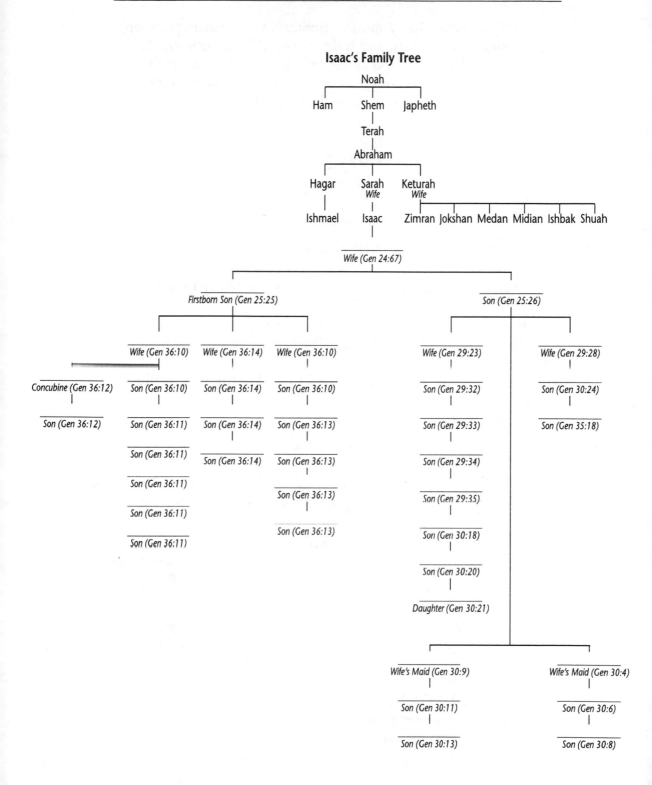

All right! Now that you have finished your lunch, pack up, climb back into the raft, and hold on tight! Two very tough rapids—Tablesaw and the awesome Hell's Hole—are right down the river. Don't forget to practice saying your memory verse three times in a row, three times today!

Day Five

A PRICELESS GIFT

"Okay," Mr. Burt called out, "is everyone ready to head back into the river?"

"We sure are!" Max, Molly, Alex, and Lauren shouted.

"Then hop in," instructed Mr. Burt. "Start paddling nice and steady."

"I can hear the roar," Alex called out. "We must be getting close."

"Look ahead," Lauren yelled as the raft approached the white water. "I see a rapid!"

"Okay, guys," George reminded everyone, "look for the *V* in the water and aim for it."

"Piece of cake," Max yelled out over the roar of the water just as their raft started picking up speed and zipping down the river.

Max yelled, "Yee-ha!" as their raft hit the drop-off and lifted up into the air,

then bounced and rocked into the churning water. As they hit the water, the raft turned sideways and a huge, freezing wave washed over the side, soaking them. Then they smacked against a boulder and almost lost Lauren as she flew out of her seat.

"Whew, that was close," Lauren smiled as she climbed back into her seat. "I thought I was gone for sure that time."

Just as soon as they got their raft moving back into the river, Mr. Burt looked back and smiled. "Hear that roar? This is the big one. There are two drop-offs. If you get tossed out, just remember to turn over on your back and float with your feet first. Don't panic. Work toward the side to the quiet water. We're getting ready to go. Is everybody ready? Here it comes!"

As the raft hit the first drop-off, all you could hear was screaming as the kids bounced up and the raft hit the water to swirl around in the wild water, and then hit the second drop-off.

The raft came down, and Max shot over the side of the raft, yelling as he hit the water. He went under, swallowed a mouthful of water, and flipped. Finally he managed to break the surface of the water gasping for air. As his feet hit a rock, he remembered to flip on his back and float feet first. Just as he started floating, he spotted the raft up ahead, proceeding into the quiet water.

Max floated toward the quiet water, trying to head for the bank. Mr. Burt and his dad were already there, ready to pull him out of the river where everyone was waiting. "Now that was a ride!" Max laughed as he struggled out of the river. "Let's do that again!"

"Not right now," Max's dad smiled back. "You took about ten years off my life watching you fly out of the raft."

Mr. Burt laughed. "Let's dry off and have a snack before we head back to the outpost. Why don't you get your maps out and see how far we have to go? Then we can snack on trail mix and find out more about Jacob, Esau, and the birthright."

"That's a great idea," replied Mr. Luke. "Let's dry off and head back to Genesis."

Yesterday you discovered that Rebekah has two sons who will be two different nations, and that the older would serve the younger.

WHO is the older, the firstborn? _____

WHO is the younger? _____

WHAT did Esau sell to Jacob? His _____

WHAT is a birthright? Do you know? Let's find out what it is, and if it is important. First let's turn to page 170. Read Genesis 25:25-34. Make a list below of what you learn about the birthright in this passage in Genesis.

Birthright
Genesis 25:31-32   _ _ _ _'s birthright. _____   wanted to buy it.
Genesis 25:33   Esau _____ his _____   to _____.
Genesis 25:34   Esau _____ his birthright.
Hebrews 12:16   Esau _____ his own _____   for a _____ _____.

Now let's find out more about the birthright by doing some cross-referencing. WHAT is *cross-referencing?* Cross-referencing is where we compare Scripture with Scripture by going to other passages in the Bible. This is a very important Bible study tool that we can use as we search out the meaning of Scripture because we know that Scripture never contradicts Scripture.

Let's read Hebrews 12:14-17 printed out below.

Mark the key word *birthright* by drawing an orange box around it and coloring it green.

Then add what you learn about the birthright in Hebrews to your chart on page 34.

Hebrews 12:14-17

14 Pursue peace with all men, and the sanctification without which no one will see the Lord.

15 See to it that no one comes short of the grace of God; that no root of bitterness springing up causes trouble, and by it many be defiled;

16 that there be no immoral or godless person like Esau, who sold his own birthright for a single meal.

17 For you know that even afterwards, when he desired to inherit the blessing, he was rejected, for he found no place for repentance, though he sought for it with tears.

Now let's ask the 5 W's and an H to see what Hebrews tells us about Esau.

Hebrews 12:16 HOW is Esau described?

Hebrews 12:17 WHAT did Esau desire afterwards?

_____

WHAT do we see happen? Did Esau inherit the blessing?

_____

From WHAT you have read in Genesis 25 and Hebrews 12, WHAT do you think the birthright is? Do you know?

Write out what you think it is on the line below.

_____

Do you think it was valuable? _____ WHY or WHY not?

_____

WHICH brother thought the birthright was valuable?

_____

WHICH brother despised it? _____

Now find out what the birthright is. HOW can you find out? To get started, you can do a word study on the word *birthright*. A word study is where you look at the word you are studying in the original language in which it was written. Did you know that the Old Testament (where Genesis 25 is found) was written primarily in Hebrew with some Aramaic? And the New Testament (where Hebrews is found) was written in Koine Greek.

By looking at both the Hebrew (Old Testament) and Greek (New Testament) words for *birthright,* you will understand more about what the word *birthright* means.

Check out Max and Molly's "map" below to discover the Hebrew and Greek words for *birthright* and what they mean. And since you also discovered that Esau despised his birthright, find out what *despised* means, too!

- The Hebrew word for *birthright* is *bekowrah* (pronounced bek-o-raw), and it means "the firstling of man or beast, the firstborn; the right of the firstborn."

- The Greek word for *birthright* is *prototokia* (pronounced pro-tot-ok-ee-ah), and it means "as a privilege, a birthright."

- The Hebrew word for *despised* is *bazah* (pronounced baw-zaw), and it means "to disesteem, to not put the proper value on."

Now that you know that the birthright is a privilege that belongs to the firstborn, and that Esau, Isaac's firstborn, did not put the proper value on the birthright, let's do some more cross-referencing to get the facts about the firstborn and help you understand the importance of the birthright.

Solve the crossword puzzle on page 38 by looking up the passages of Scripture in your map (the Bible) and asking the 5 W's and an H questions.

Look up and read Genesis 49:2-4.

Genesis 49:3 WHAT do we learn about the firstborn by looking at Reuben, Jacob's firstborn?

1. (Across) My _____ and the beginning of my

2. (Down) _____. He is preeminent in 3. (Down)

_____ and 4. (Down) _____.

Do you know what it means to be preeminent? It means to have more, to be superior to or stand out above all others. Because Reuben is the firstborn, he is the beginning of Jacob's strength and might. He is to have more dignity and power than his brothers, but does he? Look at verse 4. Will he have preeminence? No. Because Reuben sins against his father, he will not have the birthright, even though he is the firstborn.

Look up and read 2 Chronicles 21:1-3.

2 Chronicles 21:3 WHAT did Jehoshaphat give Jehoram, his firstborn?

5. (Down) The _____

2 Chronicles 21:3 WHAT did he give the other children?

6. (Across) Many _____ of 7. (Down)

_____,

8. (Down) _____, and precious things with fortified cities in Judah.

Look up and read Exodus 4:22-23.

Exodus 4:22 WHO is God's firstborn?

9. (Across) _____ (This is referring to the nation.)

Look up and read Exodus 13:2,11-15.

Exodus 13:2 WHAT belongs to God?

10. (Across) The _____

Exodus 13:2 WHAT are they to do with the firstborn?

11. (Across) _____ to Me

Exodus 13:12 WHAT is the firstborn, male or female?

12. (Across) _____

Look up and read Deuteronomy 21:15-17.

Deuteronomy 21:17 WHAT does the firstborn receive?
WHAT is the firstborn's right?

13. (Across) A _____ 14. (Across) _____
of all that he has.

Look up and read Colossians 1:15-18.

Colossians 1:15 WHO is the firstborn of creation? WHO
is the "He" in this verse? If you aren't sure who the "He"
is, look back at verses 13-14. WHO is God's beloved Son
in whom we have redemption of sins?

15. (Down) _____

Colossians 1:18 WHAT else is Jesus also the firstborn of?

16. (Across) The firstborn from the _____

This doesn't mean that Jesus was the first person who was raised from the dead, because we know that Jesus raised Lazarus from the dead before He died on the cross. But this means that Jesus is the first to have ever been raised from the dead to never die again!

Jesus is alive! He lives in heaven with the Father, and one day He will come back and take you to live in heaven with Him, never to die again, if you have accepted Him as your Savior.

Do you see how important the birthright was? The birthright belonged to the firstborn (the first male child). The firstborn was the beginning of the father's might and strength. He was to receive a double portion of the inheritance, and if the father had a kingdom, it was to go to the firstborn.

The birthright was very, very important! But HOW did Esau treat it? As if it had no value. Esau cared more about satisfying his hunger than about the inheritance that belonged to him. Esau was not looking at future blessings but only at his needs of the moment.

mmmmm!

He did not control his appetite but gave in to his desires and gave up his inheritance for a bowl of stew. Isn't that sad? Do you remember how he was described in Hebrews? He was an immoral and godless person who later desired to inherit the blessing but was rejected. There was no repentance (a changing of the mind), only tears.

HOW about you? Do you know that you have a birthright if you have accepted Jesus Christ as your Savior? Once you

have accepted Jesus, you are a child of God and share in His inheritance (Colossians 3:24; 1 Peter 1:3-4).

Are you like Esau? Do you value your inheritance in Jesus Christ, or is it worthless to you? Are you living for God's kingdom, or for the world in which you live? HOW do you know? Examine your heart and the things you do.

- Do you obey God and do what His Word says?

_____

- Do you share the gospel, even if it means kids will laugh and make fun of you?

_____

- Do you have self-control? Do you watch television shows you shouldn't watch, look at bad things on the Internet, and say words that you shouldn't say because all of your friends do?

  Write out what you do below.

  _____

- Do you live for the moment, caught up in your feelings and desires, or do you think about your future? Example: Will you wait until you are married to have a physical relationship, like God's Word says, or will you allow yourself to get caught up in what you are feeling at the moment?

  Write out what you will do on the line below

  _____

  Would you steal something you wanted, or would you wait until you could buy it?

  Write out what you would do on the line below.

  _____

  Would you take drugs if someone promised they would make you feel good to satisfy that need at the moment, or would you say no and trust God to get you through?

  _____

Remember, you are a child of God. You have an inheritance that is waiting for you in heaven. If you value it, then you will want to live the way God tells you to by doing what He says is right, whether it is easy or not. Your friends may make fun of you, ignore you, and reject you. But you have to decide how much you value God. Is your birthright important to you?

As we close today, spend some time with God, thanking Him for the priceless birthright He has given you. Ask Him how He wants you to live to honor this priceless gift. Ask Him to help you stand firm when you are lonely and rejected. Remember how He answered Isaac and Rebekah. He hears your prayers, and He will answer you!

Way to go! You did an awesome job! Now that you have dried off, hop back into the raft and head down the river to the outpost. Don't forget to practice your memory verse!

2

A STOLEN BLESSING

GENESIS 26–27

That was quite an adventure last week as you learned how to read white water and ride the rapids. How do you like your extreme adventure so far? Pretty cool, isn't it? This week as you continue to explore the great outdoors, you will follow Isaac, Esau, and Jacob to discover WHAT it means to be blessed by God.

Day One

GOD'S CHOICE

"Hey, how's it going?" Mr. Burt called out as he walked up to the campsite. "Are you worn out from riding the rapids, or are you ready to head out on a new adventure this week?"

"We're ready!" Max, Molly, Alex, and Lauren replied.

"What's next?" Max asked Mr. Burt as he took a seat next to his dad.

"How does a hike across the mountains and through the forests sound?"

"Awesome!" Alex exclaimed. "Will it be just a day hike, or will we camp up there, too?"

Mr. Burt laughed as he answered Alex. "It's going to be quite a long hike. So we're going to pack up everything and camp along the way."

"Yippee!" squealed Molly. "Is George coming, too?"

"She sure is," replied Mr. Burt. "We thought you girls would like to have another girl to hang out with in your tent. You need to get some rest today, wash anything you will need, plan your supplies, and enjoy the campfire tonight. We'll head out tomorrow at first light."

"All right," said Lauren. "We'll be ready."

As Lauren answered Mr. Burt, Sam jumped out of Max's arms and jumped up on Mr. Burt, licking his face.

"Hey, what's up, fellow?" Mr. Burt asked.

"Sam's worried that we might leave him behind again," Max laughed.

"No way," replied Mr. Burt. "We need the great detective beagle as we hike through the woods. We just couldn't take you rafting, boy. We might have lost you to the rapids."

Max called Sam over and put him back in his lap. "Did you hear that, boy? You're going, too." Sam reached up and gave Max's face a good licking. Then he jumped down and ran around the campsite, sharing his excitement by jumping on Alex, Molly, and Lauren and licking their faces, too.

"Yuck," squealed Lauren as Sam jumped out of her lap. But Sam just sat on his haunches, panting and wagging his tail, proud of catching everybody off guard.

How about you? Are you ready for the big hike? Great. Before we start making our supply list, let's pick up our adventure with Isaac, Esau, and Jacob. Have you talked to your Expert Guide today? Have you prayed? Great! Then let's head out.

Last week we discovered that the birthright belonged to the firstborn son, and how Esau, Isaac's firstborn, despised his birthright. Before we move on to Genesis 26, let's take a look at one more passage of Scripture that shows just who is in control of the birthright, the inheritance, and the descendants.

Do you remember the prophecy that God told Rebekah when the children were still in her womb? Did God know WHO was going to be born first? Of course He did!

WHO did God say would be stronger?

_____

WHO would serve WHOM?

_____

Now let's compare what we know to another passage of Scripture. Read Romans 9:7-16 printed out on page 49 and mark the following key words:

God (draw a purple triangle and color it yellow)

Jacob (circle it in blue)

Esau (color it red)

choice (color it orange)

Romans 9:7-16

7 nor are they all children because they are Abraham's descendants, but: "through Isaac your descendants will be named."

8 That is, it is not the children of the flesh who are children of God, but the children of the promise are regarded as descendants.

9 For this is the word of promise: "At this time I will come, and Sarah shall have a son."

10 And not only this, but there was Rebekah also, when she had conceived twins by one man, our father Isaac;

11 for though the twins were not yet born and had not done anything good or bad, so that God's purpose according to His choice would stand, not because of works but because of Him who calls,

12 it was said to her, "The older will serve the younger."

13 Just as it is written, "Jacob I loved, but Esau I hated."

14 What shall we say then? There is no injustice with God, is there? May it never be!

15 For He says to Moses, "I will have mercy on whom I have mercy, and I will have compassion on whom I have compassion."

16 So then it does not depend on the man who wills or the man who runs, but on God who has mercy.

Did you recognize Romans 9:11? It's last week's memory verse. Now let's get the facts. In Romans 9:11-12 we see that Rebekah's twins who were not yet born had not done anything good or bad.

So WHAT is the reason that the older will serve the younger?

So that God's _____ according to His

_____ would stand, not because of _____

but because of Him who _____

Romans 9:16 WHAT does it depend on?

God who has _____

Isn't that awesome? God is the One who chooses. Before the twins were ever born, God told Rebekah that He had chosen the older to serve the younger. Jacob, the younger son, would be the stronger one through whom all the covenant promises would be fulfilled, instead of the usual firstborn son, simply because he was God's choice.

This shows us that God is a sovereign God. *Sovereign* means God is the one who is in control. He is the Ruler over all. God is a loving and compassionate God, but because He is God, it's His choice to make, not man's. Not only does God make and fulfill promises, but He also chooses who will receive the promises. God alone chooses for His will and His purpose.

Now that we have seen just how awesome our God is, let's get started on the next part of our adventure today by reading Genesis 26. Turn to your Observation Worksheet on page 171. Read Genesis 26 and mark the following key words:

God (draw a purple triangle and color it yellow)

Abraham (color it blue)

descendants (draw a blue star of David)

bless (blessing, blessed) (put a blue cloud around it and color it pink)

altar (box it in red)

covenant, oath (box it in yellow and color it red)

Esau (color it red)

Don't forget to mark anything that tells you WHERE by double-underlining the WHERE in green. And don't forget to mark anything that tells you WHEN by drawing a green clock like this:

All right! Way to go! Now discover this week's memory verse by looking at Mr. Burt's map on page 52. Use the letter and number pair under each blank. Then go to the map and find the letter, such as D at the top of the map. Then look on the left side until you find the number that goes with the D, such as 4. Find the mixed-up word in the square on the map that goes with D4, unscramble the word, and write the correct word on the blank. Do the same thing for each blank until you have discovered your verse for the week.

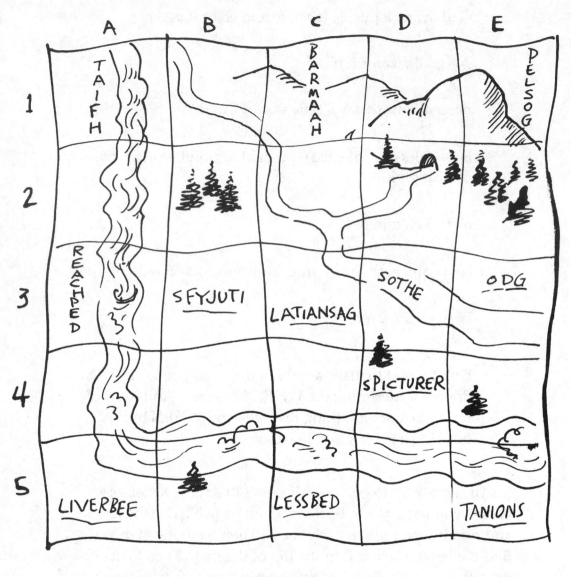

The _____, foreseeing that _____
               D4   E3

would _____ the Gentiles by _____,
         B3   A1

_____ the _____ beforehand to
   A3   E1

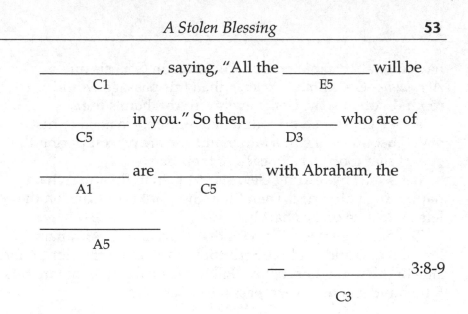

_____, saying, "All the _____ will be
C1   E5

_____ in you." So then _____ who are of
C5   D3

_____ are _____ with Abraham, the
A1   C5

_____
A5

—_____ 3:8-9
C3

Fantastic! Now don't forget to practice saying this verse three times in a row, three times today. Tomorrow we will take a closer look at Abraham and his son Isaac to see how much they are alike, and to find out about God's promise to each one.

Day Two

LiKE FATHER, LiKE SON

Rise and shine! Are you ready to head out on our big hike? Do you have your food, sleeping bag, tent, clothes, and water? Then lace up those hiking boots and put on your backpack as we put Sam on his leash and head up the trail. Don't forget your map, and remember to consult with your Expert Guide. Then we're ready to hike.

As you marked your key words in Genesis 26 yesterday, did this passage of Scripture sound familiar to you? If you have already completed our adventure in Genesis on *Abraham—God's Brave Explorer,* then this passage would remind you of some of the events in Abraham's life.

As we get started on today's adventure, we need to discover just how alike this father and son are by comparing the events that took place in each of their lives.

Let's start by reading Genesis 26 again to find out what is happening with Isaac. Then fill in the blanks for Isaac on the left-hand side of the chart below.

To compare Isaac's life with that of his father, Abraham, let's look up and read the Scripture passages on the right-hand side of the same chart below. Fill in the blanks to compare this father and son from each passage of Scripture.

ISAAC	ABRAHAM
Genesis 26:1-2 There was a _____ in the land. Isaac went to _____ because the Lord told him to not go down to _____.	Genesis 12:10 There was a _____ in the land, so Abram went down to _____. Genesis 20:1 Abram sojourned in _____.
Genesis 26:6-7 Isaac tells Abimelech's men his wife, Rebekah, is his _____.	Genesis 20:2 Abraham tells Abimelech that Sarah is his _____.
Genesis 26:7 Isaac did this because he was _____ they might _____ him.	Genesis 20:11 Abraham did this because he thought there was no _____ of God in that place and that they would _____ him.
Genesis 26:11 Abimelech charged the people, saying, "He who	

ISAAC	ABRAHAM
_____ this man or his _____ shall surely be put to _____." Genesis 26:2-3 The _____ appeared to Isaac and said, "I will be _____ you and _____ you, for to you and your _____ I will give all these _____, and I will establish the _____ which I swore to your father Abraham." Genesis 26:4 God told Isaac, "I will _____ your _____ as the _____ of heaven; and by your descendants all the _____ of the earth shall be _____."	Genesis 20:14 Abimelech r _ _ _ _ _ _ d Abraham's wife Sarah to him. Genesis 12:7 The _____ appeared to Abram and said, "To your _____ I will give this _____." Abram built an _____ to the Lord. Genesis 15:18 The Lord made a _____ with Abram, saying "To your _____ I have given this _____." Genesis 12:3 God told Abram, "I will _____ those who _____ you, and the one who _____ you I will _____. Genesis 22:17 God promised, "I will greatly _____ you, and I will greatly _____ your seed as the _____ of the heavens and as the _____ which is on the seashore."

ISAAC	ABRAHAM
Genesis 26:18 Isaac dug the _____ of _____ which had been dug in the days of Abraham, his father. Genesis 26:26-28 Abimelech came to Isaac and said, "The Lord has been _____ you…. Let there now be an _____ between us…. Let us make a _____ with you." Genesis 26:30-31 Isaac made them a _____. They ate and drank, and in the morning they exchanged _____.	Genesis 21:25 Abraham complained to Abimelech because of the _____ of _____ which the servants of Abimelech had seized. Genesis 21:22 Abimelech told Abraham, "God is _____ you in all you do." Genesis 21:27 Abraham and Abimelech made a _____. Genesis 21:31 He called the place Beersheba, because the two of them took an _____.

Wow! Are you amazed to see how many of the events in Abraham's and Isaac's lives are exactly the same? Does it surprise you to see Isaac making the same mistake as his father did when he encountered King Abimelech? The son had the same fears as his father.

Now, let's take a look at Esau.

Genesis 26:34 HOW old is Esau? _____ years old

Do you remember HOW old Isaac was when he had Jacob and Esau? If you don't, go back to Genesis 25:26 and find out.

HOW old was Isaac when Esau was born?

_____ years old

So if Esau is now 40 years old, HOW old is Isaac?

_____ years old

Genesis 26:34 WHO are the two girls that Esau married?

_____ the daughter of _____ the Hittite

and _____ the daughter of _____ the

Hittite

Genesis 26:35 WHAT did this do to Isaac and Rebekah?

_____

Isn't that sad? Esau takes wives from the Hittites and brings grief to his parents. Do you remember how his dad, Isaac, got his wife?

HOW should you choose the girl or boy that you will marry one day?

_____

Now let's see what we can discover about God and His character.

Genesis 26:1-3 To WHOM is God promising the land?

_____

So is God a covenant-keeping God? Did He keep His

promise to Abraham that the land would belong to his

descendants? _____

WHAT else do we learn about God? Look for the key

word in Genesis 26:3, 4, 12, 24, and 29. WHAT does the

Lord do to Isaac and to all the nations of the earth? He

b __ __ __ __ __ s.

   Awesome! God shows us He is a faithful God who keeps
His promises, and that He is a God of blessings.
   Why don't you take a few minutes to thank God for WHO
He is and what He has done for you? Write out a short prayer
of praise to your covenant-keeping God on the lines below.

_____

_____

_____

_____

   We will find out more about the blessings and being blessed
later. Don't forget to practice saying your memory verse!

Day Three

DECEPTION AND LIES

"Oh look, there's a stream," Molly called out. "Does the trail lead us through the water?"

"It sure does," George replied.

"I like hopping from rock to rock," Lauren called out to Molly. "Look at Sam! He's drinking the water."

"Come on, Sam. Stay with us, boy," Mr. Burt called out. "We should be coming to a small clearing soon. Then we will take a break and have some lunch. After lunch I have a little surprise for you."

"What?" asked Max.

George laughed as she answered. "You're just going to have to wait to find out."

"Oh, man," Alex replied. "What kind of surprise could there be out here in the middle of a forest? Oh look, there's a deer! Do you see it, Max?"

"Awesome! This is so cool! Can we go up ahead and explore, Mr. Burt?"

"Sure, just follow the marked trail. And keep an eye out for the clearing. It's about another mile up the trail."

As Max and Alex reached the clearing, they started setting up for lunch while waiting for the others to catch up. "Here they come," Alex called out. "Hey, guys, we're ready to eat."

"So are we," answered Molly. "Let's finish unpacking the food and eat."

After everyone was finished, Mr. Luke said, "Let's pull out our maps and find out what is happening in our extreme adventure with God."

Let's pray. Then we need to head to Genesis 27 on page 174. Read Genesis 27 and mark the following key words:

Lord (God) (draw a purple triangle and color it yellow)

Esau (color it red)

Jacob (circle it in blue)

bless (blessing, blessed) (put a blue cloud around it and color it pink)

birthright (box it in orange and color it green)

curse (box it in orange and color it brown)

Don't forget to mark anything that tells you WHERE by double-underlining the WHERE in green. And don't forget to mark anything that tells you WHEN by drawing a green clock like this:

Let's find out what is happening in Genesis 27 by asking the 5 W's and an H.

WHO are the main characters?

_____

Genesis 27:1-4 WHAT does Isaac want to do before he dies?

_____

Genesis 27:5-17 WHAT does Rebekah want to happen?

_____

Genesis 27:9-17 WHAT is Rebekah's plan?

(verse 9) "Go bring me _____ choice young

_____ so I can prepare a _____ dish for your

_____ that he loves." (verse 15) She

took the best _____ of Esau

and put them on _____. (verse 16)

She put the _____ of the young

goats on his _____ and on the

smooth part of his _____.

HOW is Rebekah behaving?
Circle one of the answers.

   a. She is honest with Isaac.

   b. She is deceiving Isaac and Esau.

WHY would Rebekah do this since she already knows God's promise? Is she trying to help God out? Do you remember Sarah's heartache with Hagar when she tried to help God out?

Does God need our help, or should we be patient and wait on Him?

_____

Genesis 27:12 WHAT is Jacob's concern?

_____

Does Jacob go along with Rebekah's plan?

_____ Yes _____ No

Genesis 27:19, 24 Does Jacob lie to his father?

_____

Genesis 27:27-30 WHO gets the blessing?

_____

Genesis 27:30-31 WHAT happens?

_____

Genesis 27:34-35 When Esau cries for a blessing, WHAT is Isaac's response?

_____

Genesis 27:36 WHAT does Esau say about Jacob?

_____

_____

Is this statement about the birthright the truth? _____

WHAT really happened?

_____

Genesis 27:41 HOW did Esau feel about Jacob? WHAT did he plan to do when Isaac died?

_____

Genesis 27:42-45 WHAT is Rebekah's plan?

_____

Genesis 27:44 HOW long does Rebekah plan for Jacob to be away?

_____

Genesis 27:46 HOW is Rebekah able to get away with sending Jacob away? WHAT does she tell Isaac?

_____

Isn't this a sad story? Did you notice how deceptive Rebekah was? She lied to her husband, Isaac, and to her son Esau.

Is it ever okay to lie? _____ No way! Lying is a sin.

Rebekah chooses to do the wrong thing, and because of her deception she loses her favorite son. She has to send Jacob away so that Esau won't kill him. Instead of being gone for a few days as she planned, Jacob was gone for 20 years (Genesis 31:41). And Genesis doesn't say if she ever got to see him again.

Jacob did get the blessing, but we know the reason he received the blessing wasn't because of the deception, but because it was God's choice from the very beginning. Rebekah needed to trust and wait on God. God always does what He says He will do.

We also see that we are responsible when we sin. Just look at how Isaac's whole family suffered because of a craving, choosing favorites, deception, and fear. Esau lost his birthright because of his craving, and Rebekah lost her son because of her favoritism, deception, and fears.

HOW about you? Are you deceptive? Do you lie to get your way? Have you ever tricked your mother, father, brother, or sister? Have you lied to them about something you did or didn't do?

Write out what you did on the lines below.

_____

_____

_____

The next time you are tempted to lie, remember Jacob and Esau. Tell the truth and trust that God is in control and has the very best plans for you!

Way to go! We will learn more about the blessing of Jacob and Esau tomorrow.

Day Four

jacob aNd esau's blessiNg

"Okay, we're ready for our surprise," Max said.

George, Mr. Burt, Mr. Luke, and Mr. Paul all laughed. Mr. Paul spoke up. "You better show them before you have a mutiny on your hands."

"Okay, guys. Walk over to the side of that big rock. How would you like to learn how to rock climb?"

"Really?" asked Max. "How? We don't have any gear."

"Yes, you do," replied Mr. Luke. "Mr. Paul and I have all your gear, so unpack and get ready to climb."

A few minutes later, wearing helmets, climbing shoes, and harnesses, the kids were ready for their first lesson. Mr. Burt told the kids, "We're going to start on this small rock so that you don't have very far to go if you fall. Use your hands and fingers for a hold on each ledge, bump, or crack. You've got it. Keep practicing. Later I will show you how to use the ropes."

After an hour of learning to climb, Mr. Burt called for a short rest. "We need to rest and have a snack so that we can get back on the trail. We'll do more climbing later."

Let's pray. Then pull out your maps. Let's find out the details of Jacob's and Esau's blessings.

Do you know what it means to bless? Take a look at Max and Molly's map on page 66.

> The Hebrew word for *bless* is *barak* (pronounced baw–rak). It means "to kneel, to bless God as an act of adoration, to bless man as a benefit."

Let's head back to page 174. Read Genesis 27. Fill in the blanks below to make a list describing the details of Jacob's and Esau's blessings.

JACOB	ESAU
Genesis 27:28 May God give you the _____ of _____, _____ of the earth, an _____ of _____ and _____. Genesis 27:29 May peoples _____ you, and _____ _____ _____ to you. Be _____ of your _____. May your mother's _____ _____ _____ to you. _____ be those who _____ you, and _____ be those who _____ you.	Genesis 27:39 You will dwell away from the _____ of the earth and _____ of _____ above. Genesis 27:40 You shall live by your _____ and _____ your brother. When you become restless, you will _____ his _____ from your neck.

Do you understand these blessings? WHAT does it mean for Jacob to have the dew of heaven, the fatness of the earth, and an abundance of grain and new wine? It means that the earth would be fertile, and that he would have an abundance of food.

We also see that many peoples and nations will bow down to and serve Jacob. All of his brothers will bow down to him, and anyone who curses him will be cursed, and those who bless him will be blessed.

WHAT does Esau's blessing mean, since it says Esau will dwell away from the earth's fertility? Does that sound like his land will be fertile and grow an abundance of food?

_____ Yes _____ No

WHAT does it sound like to you?

_____

Do you know what it means to live by the sword? Esau will be in conflict with other people. HOW about breaking the yoke of his brother? A yoke is a symbol of bondage and servitude.

WHO is going to serve WHOM?

_____

Esau will get restless and break free from serving his brother.

Why don't you draw a picture of Jacob's and Esau's blessings in the boxes below to help you remember them?

Jacob's Blessing	Esau's Blessing

WHO gives the blessings? WHAT kinds of blessings are there? Let's find out by looking up and reading the following Scripture passages.

Genesis 12:1-3 WHO is blessing Abram?

_____

Genesis 12:3 HOW will all the families of the earth be blessed?

_____

Genesis 17:14-16 WHO blesses Sarah?

_____

Genesis 17:16 WHAT is Sarah's blessing?

_____

Genesis 17:20 HOW will God bless Ishmael?

_____

Genesis 22:17 HOW will God bless Abraham?

_____

Genesis 26:1-4 WHOM is God blessing?

_____

Genesis 26:3-4 WHAT is his blessing?

"To you and to your _____ I will give all

these _____, and I will establish the _____

which I swore to your father Abraham. I will

_____ your descendants as the _____ of

heaven…and by your descendants all the _____

of the earth shall be blessed."

Genesis 27:28 As Isaac blesses Jacob, WHOM does he ask
to bless Jacob?

"May _____ give you of the dew of heaven."

So WHO gave all these blessings we just looked up?

_____

WHAT kinds of blessings did you see?

_____

_____

Are there blessings for you and me? We will find out
tomorrow as we continue our expedition. Now don't forget to
practice saying your memory verse.

Day Five

GOD'S BLESSING FOR YOU

"Hey," Max called back to Mr. Burt, "this trail is getting pretty narrow. Are we setting up camp in the middle of the woods?"

"No, in a couple of miles it will begin to flatten out, and we'll find a great spot for our campsite. Are you getting tired?"

"A little bit," Max answered, "but mostly hungry." Sam started yapping his agreement, and Mr. Burt laughed. "Hiking and climbing make you awfully hungry. Why don't you get some "gorp" out of your bag and eat it on the way?"

"What's "gorp"?" Molly asked.

"It's your trail mix," answered George. "We call it "gorp" to stand for good old raisins and peanuts."

"That's pretty cool," Molly replied. "Oh look, over there. I think I saw something moving through the forest."

"Yeah," Alex whispered to Molly, "a big, old bear looking for his snack."

Molly swatted at Alex. "That's not funny. I did see something."

George laughed. "It was probably another deer, or maybe it was a raccoon. Keep your eyes open. There's a lot of wildlife around here."

As they continued to hike up the trail, they spotted a few birds and a chipmunk that Sam decided needed a good chase. Just as Sam was settling back in and panting next to Max, George called out that they had arrived at their destination for the night. They all scouted around until they found just the right spot and started setting up camp.

"This is an awesome spot, Mr. Burt," said Max as he looked out over the ridge. "Look at all those mountains. Look how high up we are. This is so cool."

"I love this place," Molly sighed. "When do we eat?"

"As soon as you fix it," laughed George. "We'll get everything ready while you guys explore your map. Then you get to cook, and we'll clean up. How does that sound for teamwork?"

"Sounds great," replied Lauren. "Let's get out our maps. Why don't you pray today, Alex? Then we're ready for our next adventure in God's Word."

Are you ready to see if God has a blessing for you and me? Yesterday as we took a closer look at Jacob's and Esau's blessings, we also saw the blessings that God bestowed on Abraham, Sarah, Ishmael, and Isaac. Isn't it awesome to see that God is the Giver of the blessings? Do you think that God has a blessing for you and me? Let's find out. Turn to page 203. Read Acts 3:1–4:4 and mark the following key words:

Jesus (draw a purple cross and color it yellow)

faith (believed) (draw a purple book and color it green)

bless (blessing, blessed) (put a blue cloud around it and color it pink)

Abraham (color it blue)

covenant (box it in yellow and color it red)

Now answer the 5 W's and an H questions.

Acts 3:2 WHAT do we discover about the man?

He was _____.

Acts 3:6 WHAT did Peter tell the man to do in the name

of Jesus Christ the Nazarene? _____

Acts 3:7-8 Was he healed? _____

Acts 3:16 WHOSE name did Peter tell the men of Israel

had strengthened the lame man and given him perfect

health? _____

Acts 3:13-14 WHAT did they do to God's servant Jesus?

They _____ and _____ Him in the

presence of Pilate.

Acts 3:15 WHAT did they do to the Prince of life?

Put him to _____

Acts 3:15 WHAT did God do?

_____ Him from the dead

Acts 3:19 WHAT does Peter want them to do so their sins

may be wiped away? _____ and _____

Acts 3:25 WHAT was the covenant that God made with Abraham?

"In your _____ all the _____ of the _____

shall be _____."

Acts 3:26 HOW did God send Jesus to bless them?

By turning them from their _____ _____

Acts 4:4 WHAT happened to many who heard the message?

They _____.

Now let's discover more about this blessing. Read Galatians 3:5-14 printed out on pages 75-76, and mark the following key words:

Christ (Christ Jesus) (draw a purple cross and color it yellow)

Spirit (draw a purple symbol and color it yellow)

bless (blessing, blessed) (put a blue cloud around it and color it pink)

Abraham (color it blue)

curse (box it in orange and color it brown)

gospel (draw a red megaphone and color it green)

faith (draw a purple book and color it green)

Galatians 3:5-14

5 So then, does He who provides you with the Spirit and works miracles among you, do it by the works of the Law, or by hearing with faith?

6 Even so Abraham believed God, and it was reckoned to him as righteousness.

7 Therefore, be sure that it is those who are of faith who are sons of Abraham.

8 The Scripture, foreseeing that God would justify the Gentiles by faith, preached the gospel beforehand to Abraham, saying, "All the nations will be blessed in you."

9 So then those who are of faith are blessed with Abraham, the believer.

10 For as many as are of the works of the Law are under a curse; for it is written, "Cursed is everyone who does not abide by all things written in the book of the law, to perform them."

11 Now that no one is justified by the Law before God is evident; for, "The righteous man shall live by faith."

12 However, the Law is not of faith; on the contrary, "He who practices them shall live by them."

13 Christ redeemed us from the curse of the Law, having become a curse for us—for it is written, "Cursed is everyone who hangs on a tree"—

14 in order that in Christ Jesus the blessing of Abraham might come to the Gentiles, so that we would receive the promise of the Spirit through faith.

Discover the blessing. Ask the 5 W's and an H.

Galatians 3:8 WHAT did God preach to Abraham?

The _____

Do you know what the gospel is? The word *gospel* means "good news," and it is the good news that Jesus Christ, the Son of God, came into the world to die on the cross to save sinners like you and me! Jesus died and was buried, but He rose again on the third day, never to die again. Isn't that *awesome?*

Galatians 3:9 WHO are blessed with Abraham the believer?

Those who are of _____

Galatians 3:14 HOW does the blessing of Abraham come to the Gentiles?

In _____ _____ (circle together as one word in the word search)

Galatians 3:14 WHAT promise do we receive through faith?

The promise of the _____

Now go back to pages 73-77 and find all the answers that you put in the blanks from Acts and Galatians and circle them in the word search below.

S	D	E	V	E	I	L	E	B	K	F	B
U	I	E	A	R	T	H	T	I	A	F	D
S	S	H	R	E	D	E	E	S	Y	A	W
E	O	T	N	E	P	E	R	Y	R	R	B
J	W	A	D	R	V	W	S	A	E	L	L
T	N	E	F	A	M	I	L	I	E	S	E
S	E	D	T	Q	B	C	L	S	A	H	P
I	D	G	I	J	J	K	S	E	B	R	S
R	Y	N	R	U	T	E	R	K	D	U	O
H	N	Q	I	I	D	D	M	L	W	W	G
C	A	W	P	D	F	S	J	A	I	P	I
S	J	E	S	U	S	S	S	W	L	G	R

WOW! Are you amazed at your blessing? God has given you the blessing of Abraham: the free gift of salvation. Isn't that incredible? God sent His perfect Son, Jesus Christ, who never sinned, to hang on a cross and become sin for you and me so that we could receive His most precious blessing. And because Jesus paid for all our sins totally, God could raise Him from the dead. Then the blessing of Abraham could come to us when we believe, so that we could receive the promise of the Holy Spirit living in us.

Have you received the blessing of Abraham? Have you accepted Jesus Christ as your Savior? _____ If you have, then your sin has been paid for, and you have eternal life. You have the blessing of the Holy Spirit living in you.

If you have not received God's blessing of salvation, then you can receive it right now. All you have to do is come to God and ask. You need to admit that you are a sinner (Romans 3:23—"For all have sinned and fall short of the glory of God"). Tell God that you are sorry for your sins and want to be a follower of Jesus Christ.

You can pray a prayer like this:

> Thank You, God, for loving me and sending Your Son, Jesus Christ, to die for my sins. I am sorry for the things I have done wrong. I am repenting— changing my mind about my sins. Sin is wrong. I don't want to do things my way anymore. I want to receive Jesus Christ as my Savior, and now I turn my entire life over to You. Amen.

If you prayed this prayer, then you have been declared righteous just like Abraham. You are a part of God's family! You are God's child, and Jesus and the Holy Spirit will come to live in you (John 14:23). Isn't that awesome?

Now that you have become a part of God's family, you will want to share this great news by telling other people (confessing with your mouth) that you have believed in Jesus Christ and received God's blessing. You are now a child of God!

3

FAMILY TROUBLE

GENESIS 27–30

Rise and shine! Are you ready to continue our extreme adventure of following Isaac, Esau, and Jacob? Great! Then let's grab some breakfast, pull out our maps, and find out how Esau handles Jacob stealing his blessing

Day One

BROTHER TROUBLE

"Hey, guys, the campsite looks great," Mr. Burt told the kids as he completed his cleanup inspection. "We're not going to break down our campsite today because we are going on a rock-climbing adventure just a couple of miles away. Then we'll come back here to spend the night."

"All right!" exclaimed Max. "Let's go!"

As the kids arrived at their rock-climbing destination, they were in awe of the huge rock that Mr. Burt stopped in front of. "Is that the rock we're climbing, Mr. Burt?" asked Molly.

"It sure is. Don't worry. We'll be right there with you. This is going to be lots of fun. Put on your gear, and let's get ready to climb."

"Max, why don't you go first?" Mr. Burt suggested after he checked out Max's harness and equipment. "Just remember what you've learned and have fun. Okay, belay on. Climb!"

"Climbing," Max replied back as he started up the gigantic rock.

"Oh," Molly called out after she started up the rock. "This is hard and a little scary, but very, very cool!"

George laughed. "You're doing great. Just go slowly from crack to crack."

Max, Molly, Alex, Lauren, and George continued to climb as they tested their strength and endurance. After about 15 minutes, George pointed out, "Look up ahead. A few more feet and we will be ready to pull ourselves up on that ledge."

You did it! You made it to the top of the rock. Now pull yourself up, take a deep breath, and drink some water. Then get out your maps and discover what is happening with Esau now that Jacob has deceived his father and stolen the blessing.

Don't forget to pray! Then turn to Genesis 27 on page 174 to take a closer look at Esau's emotions.

Read Genesis 27:41-46.

Genesis 27:41 HOW was Esau acting in this verse? Circle the answer that best describes Esau's feelings.

a. angry but forgiving

b. angry and determined to get even

Have you ever done something out of anger or to spite

someone else? _____

WHAT did you do? Write it out below.

_____

_____

_____

Did you later regret that you did it?

_____

WHAT is Esau planning to do to Jacob when Isaac dies?

_____

Genesis 27:45 WHY does Esau want to do this? What is he feeling?

_____

The Hebrew word for *anger* in this passage is *aph* (pronounced af) and means "a nostril, nose, face, anger, from the rapid breathing in of passion, wrath." Have you ever heard the expression "in your face"? Sounds like this kind of anger, doesn't it?

which one is "angry?"

Let's look at another example of anger. Look up and read Genesis 4:4-8. The Hebrew word for *angry* in this passage is *charah* (pronounced khaw-RAW), and it means "to glow, or grow warm, to blaze up of anger, zeal, jealously, to be angry, to burn."

Genesis 4:4-6 WHO is angry in this passage?

_____

WHY is he angry?

_____

Genesis 4:7 WHAT did God tell Cain to do?

_____

WHAT is Cain to master?

_____

Did Cain sin in his anger? Look at verse 8. WHAT did Cain do?

_____

Did Cain's anger control him?

_____

Have you ever been angry with your brother or sister?

_____

HOW did you handle that anger? WHAT did you do?

_____

Let's find out how the Bible says we are to behave. Look up and read Hebrews 12:14-17.

Hebrews 12:14 WHAT are we to do?

_____

Hebrews 12:15 WHAT happens when we don't respond
the right way in difficult situations?

_____

HOW should we handle anger? Do you know? Read
Ephesians 4:25–32 printed out below. Mark the key word _anger_
(draw black squiggly lines like this: _MMM_).

Ephesians 4:25-32

25 Therefore, laying aside falsehood, speak truth each one
    of you with his neighbor, for we are members of one
    another.

26 Be angry, and yet do not sin; do not let the sun go down
    on your anger,

27 and do not give the devil an opportunity.

28 He who steals must steal no longer; but rather he must
    labor, performing with his own hands what is good, so
    that he will have something to share with one who has
    need.

29 Let no unwholesome word proceed from your mouth,
    but only such a word as is good for edification
    according to the need of the moment, so that it will give
    grace to those who hear.

30 Do not grieve the Holy Spirit of God, by whom you
    were sealed for the day of redemption.

31 Let all bitterness and wrath and anger and clamor and slander be put away from you, along with all malice.

32 Be kind to one another, tender-hearted, forgiving each other, just as God in Christ also has forgiven you.

Now ask the 5 W's and an H to solve the crossword puzzle on page 87.

Ephesians 4:25 WHAT are we to do?

1. (Across) Lay aside _____;

speak 2. (Down) _____.

Ephesians 4:26 HOW are we to deal with our anger?

3. (Down) Be angry but do not _____.

Ephesians 4:27 WHAT does our anger do?

4. (Down) Gives the _____ an 5. (Across)

_____

Ephesians 4:29 WHAT is not to come out of your mouth?

6. (Down) No _____

7. (Across)_____

Ephesians 4:29 WHAT words are to come out of your mouth?

8. (Across) A word that is good for _____

Ephesians 4:31 WHAT are we to put aside?

9. (Across) Let all _____, and

10. (Down) _____, and 11. (Down) _____ and

12. (Across) _____ and

13. (Across) _____ be put away from you along

with all 14. (Across) _____.

Ephesians 4:32 HOW are we to treat one another?

15. (Down) Be _____ to one another,

16. (Down)_____,

17. (Across)_____ each other.

WHY are we to do this?

18. (Across) Because God in _____ also has

19. (Across) _____ you

HOW did Esau deal with his anger? Was it with bitterness and malice, or did he "pursue" (that means to go after) forgiveness and peace with his brother Jacob?

Did Esau sin in his anger? _____

HOW do you handle your anger?

• Do you bear a grudge against the person you are angry with?

_____ Yes   _____ No   _____ Sometimes

• Are you controlled by your feelings? Do you yell and scream, slam doors, and say ugly things? Write out how you act when you get angry on the line below.

_____

• Do you have hateful feelings toward the person you are angry with? Do you feel bitter and want to get even, or are you kind and tenderhearted? Do you forgive?
Write out what you do on the lines below.

_____

_____

The next time you get angry, remember what you learned today. We are not to let anger rule our emotions and cause us to sin. We are to put aside all our hard feelings. We are to be kind and forgiving to each other because Jesus Christ has forgiven us for all the mean and ugly things that we have done, even though it cost Him His life. If Jesus can forgive us, then we can forgive each other, too!

Now take a minute and ask God if there is someone in your life that you have bitter and hurt feelings toward. Take a piece of paper and write down the name of that person and why you have hurt feelings and bitterness.

Then fold the paper up and ask God to help you put aside those bitter and hurt feelings. Sometimes the hurt is so bad that the only way you can forgive is to hand it over to God and tell Him you can't do it on your own, but that you know He can do it through you!

And just because you forgive someone doesn't mean that God won't punish him for what he did to you. It means that you are turning over what he did to you to God, and you will let Him be the Judge. It means that you will no longer hold his offense against him. You will let go of your feelings and set that person free.

After you have turned your hurt and anger over to God and asked Him to help you forgive that person, take the piece of paper, tear it up, and throw it away to show that you are handing it over to God. Don't give Satan an opportunity in your life. Let God have your hurt, anger, and bitterness so that you won't end up like Esau—a godless and immoral man.

Way to go! God is sooooo very proud of you!

Now, rock climbers, before you head back down the rock, solve your memory verse. Take a look at the rock wall below. As you rappel down the rocks, look at the words that are inscribed in the rocks. First you need to put an *X* over each word in the rocks that has to do with rock climbing. Then take the words that are left and place them in order on the blanks on page 91 to discover this week's verse. Once you have solved your puzzle, go back to page 85 to discover the reference for this verse.

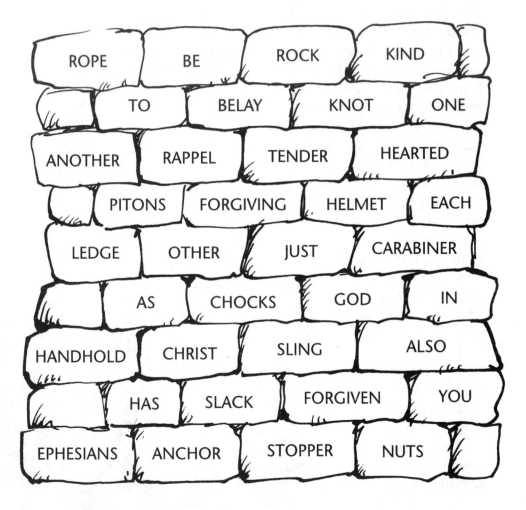

_____ _____ _____ _____ ,

_____ - _____ , _____ _____

_____ , _____ _____ _____ _____

_____ _____ _____ _____

_____ .

— _____ 4: _____

All right! Now practice saying this verse three times in a row three times today!

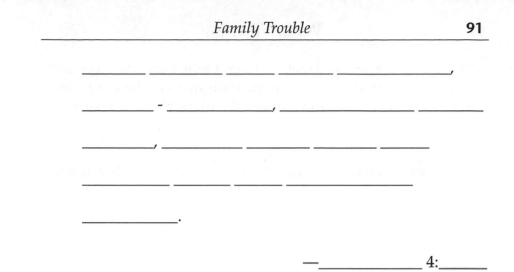

Day Two

JACOB'S DREAM

Wow! How did you like climbing that big rock? Are you a little shaky now that your feet are back on the ground? Let's hike back to the campsite and take out our maps. That was a powerful lesson yesterday on anger and forgiveness. We saw how very important it is to put aside our anger so we don't sin.

Today let's turn to page 178 to find out what happens

after Rebekah fears for Jacob's life and tells Isaac she does not want Jacob to take a wife from the daughters of the land. Don't forget to pray. Then read Genesis 28 and mark the following key words:

Lord (God) (draw a purple triangle and color it yellow)

Esau (color it red)

Jacob (circle it in blue)

bless (blessing, blessed) (put a blue cloud around it and color it pink)

dream (draw a blue cloud)

descendants (draw a blue star of David)

land (double-underline it in green and color it blue)

Don't forget to mark anything that tells you WHERE by double-underlining the WHERE in green. And don't forget to mark anything that tells you WHEN by drawing a green clock like this:

Now let's find out what is happening in Genesis 28 by asking the 5 W's and an H.

Genesis 28:1 WHAT does Isaac say to Jacob?

_____

Genesis 28:2 WHERE does Isaac tell Jacob to go?

_____

WHAT does Isaac tell Jacob to do?

_____

Genesis 28:3-4 WHAT does Isaac say to Jacob about God?

"May God Almighty _____ you and make you

_____ and _____ you, that you may

become a _____ of peoples. May He also give

you the _____ of Abraham, to you and to

your _____ with you, that you may possess the

_____ of your sojournings, which _____ gave

to Abraham."

Genesis 28:6 WHAT did Esau see?

_____

Genesis 28:8-9 WHAT did Esau do, and WHY did he do it?

_____

_____

Esau goes to Ishmael and marries his daughter Mahalath because he wants to please Isaac by taking a wife who was not from the daughters of Canaan, since he saw that the daughters of Canaan displeased his father.

Genesis 28:12 WHAT happens to Jacob after he departs from Beersheba?

He has a _____.

Genesis 28:12-15 WHAT was Jacob's dream?

_____

_____

_____

Draw a picture of this dream in the cloud below.

Genesis 28:13-15 WHAT did the Lord say to Jacob?

WHAT does He promise him? "I am the _____ ,

the God of your father _____ and the God of

_____ ; the _____ on which you lie, I will

give it to you and to your _____." (verse

14) "Your _____ will also be like the

_____ of the earth…and in your _____

shall all the families of the earth be _____."

(verse 15) "I am _____ you and will

_____ you wherever you go, and will bring you

back to this land; for I will not _____ you until I

have done what I have _____ you."

Isn't this awesome? We see God confirming the promise to Jacob that He had already made to Abraham and Isaac. God has promised not to leave Jacob until He has done what He has promised!

Genesis 28:16 WHAT did Jacob say when he woke up?

_____

Genesis 28:17 WHAT did Jacob say about this awesome place?

_____

Genesis 28:18 WHAT did Jacob do the next morning?

_____

_____

Genesis 28:19 WHAT did Jacob call the name of that place?

_____

Do you know why Jacob changed the name of that place from Luz to Bethel? It's because *Bethel* means "the house of God."

Genesis 28:20-21 WHAT is Jacob's vow?

"If _____ will be _____ me and will

_____ me on this journey that I take, and will give

me _____ to eat and _____ to wear,

and I _____ to my father's house in

_____, then the _____ will be my

_____."

Has God already promised to be with Jacob and keep

him (look back at verse 15)? _____

Genesis 28:22 WHAT was the stone that Jacob set up as a
pillar?

_____

WHAT will Jacob give to God?

Do you remember how Abraham gave Melchizedek a tenth
of all in Genesis 14? Look up and read Leviticus 27:30-32.

Leviticus 27:32 WHAT is holy to the Lord?

_____

Do you give God a part of all that
you have been given either through
your allowance or money that
you have earned?

_____

Should you? Yes! We are to give to God because it all belongs to Him. He is the Giver of all our blessings and gifts. Our tithe is holy to the Lord.

All right! Way to go! Tomorrow we will find out what happens to Jacob as he comes to the land of the sons of the east.

Day Three

jACOB AND RACHEL

"That was an awesome climb!" Max said as he and Alex were helping fix dinner.

"I hope we get to do it again," Alex replied, "although my arms are feeling pretty sore right now."

"Mine, too," Molly agreed. "Hey, where's Sam?"

"Uh-oh," Max replied. "I wonder when he wandered off. He was just here a minute ago, begging for a treat. Dad," Max called out, "can I go look for Sam?"

"Yes, but take your compass, and don't go too far. Stay on the trail, and if you don't see him in about 20 minutes, head back to the campsite. I don't want you to get caught in the woods after dark."

"Yes, sir. Mr. Paul, is it all right if Alex comes with me?"

"Sure," replied Mr. Paul. "Just be careful."

Max and Alex both headed down the trail calling for Sam.

As Alex checked his watch, he reminded Max, "It's been about 15 minutes. If we don't find him soon, we're going to have to start heading back."

"I know," Max replied. "I just can't believe he went this far. He must have caught the scent of some animal. Wait a minute. Do you hear that? I think that's Sam barking. Come on!"

Sure enough, as Max and Alex cut through the woods, they saw Sam with the fur bristling on his back, barking at a porcupine. "No, Sam!" Max called out. "Come here, boy."

But it was too late. In two seconds the porcupine turned and lifted its tail and smacked Sam right across the face. Sam yelped, his chin full of quills, and ran to Max. Max looked at Alex. "Let's hurry and get him back to Dad. He'll know what to do."

As Max and Alex raced back to the campsite with Sam, Mr. Luke heard them calling and met them on the trail. "Well, Sam, old boy, your curiosity has done it this time. Let's get the first-aid kit and pull out those quills. This is going to hurt, but he'll be okay. Let this be a lesson, Sam, old boy. Don't mess with porcupines!"

Now that Sam's adventure is over, and he is safe at the campsite, we need to pull out our maps and find out what happens as Jacob arrives in the land of the sons of the east. Turn to page 180. Read Genesis 29 and mark the following key words:

Jacob (circle it in blue)

Rachel (color it pink)

Leah (box it in green and color it green)

love (draw a red heart)

unloved (draw a red heart and put a black line through it)

deceived (box it in brown)

Underline each child's name and what his name means in blue. Then write the mother's name next to her son's in the margin.

Don't forget to mark anything that tells you WHERE by double-underlining the WHERE in green. And don't forget to mark anything that tells you WHEN by drawing a green clock like this: 🕐

Now, let's find out what happens.

Genesis 29:5 WHAT does Jacob ask the men from Haran?

_____

Genesis 29:6 WHOM do these men point out to Jacob?

_____

Genesis 29:9 WHAT is Rachel?

_____

Genesis 29:10 WHAT does Jacob do for Rachel?

_____

Genesis 29:11 WHAT does Jacob do next?

_____

Genesis 29:12 WHAT does Rachel do?

_____

Genesis 29:13-14 Does Laban receive Jacob and welcome him into his house?

_____ Yes   _____ No

Genesis 29:16-17 WHO are Laban's two daughters? Write out how they are described after you write their names.

Older daughter:

_____

Younger daughter:

_____

Have you ever felt like your brothers or sisters are prettier, better athletes, smarter, or more popular than you?

_____ Yes   _____ No   _____ Sometimes

HOW does it make you feel? Does it make you mad at them, hurt, jealous, or feel that you are just not good enough? Write out how you feel on the line below.

_____

Should you feel that way? Remember WHO created you: God! God made you special just like you are. He does not want you to compare yourself to anyone else. He made you a unique, one-of-a-kind creation, and He loves you just like you are!

Genesis 29:18 WHOM did Jacob love?

_____

WHAT did Jacob tell Laban he would do for Rachel?

_____

Wow! Isn't that amazing? Jacob is willing to serve seven years in order to marry Rachel. Tomorrow we will find out what happens when his seven years of service are up.

You are doing an awesome job roughing it in the wilderness. Keep up the good work, and don't forget to practice your memory verse!

Day Four

A DECEIVER IS DECEIVED

As Sam recovers from his great porcupine adventure today, it is time to break camp and head back toward our main campsite. Let's make sure we do a super cleanup job so that other people can enjoy these great outdoors, too! Great work! Now let's spend some time with our Expert Guide. Then we will be ready to hit the trail.

Yesterday as Jacob arrived in Haran, he met Laban, his mother's brother, and fell in love with Rachel. Because of his love for Rachel, Jacob is willing to serve Laban for seven years. Today we need to discover WHAT happens when his seven years are up. Turn to page 182. Read Genesis 29:21-35.

Now follow the trail. WHAT happens to God's chosen man?

Genesis 29:21-25 WHAT happened after Jacob served his seven years for Rachel, and he asked Laban for his wife? WHAT did Laban do?

_____

Uh-oh. Here comes trouble. It looks like Jacob, who deceived both his father and his brother, has now been deceived by Rachel's father.

Genesis 29:26 WHY did Laban say he did this?

_____

_____

Genesis 29:27 WHAT did Laban promise Jacob if he completed Leah's week? (The traditional wedding celebration at this time lasted a week. This is probably the "week" that is mentioned in this verse.)

_____

Genesis 29:24 WHO was Leah's maid?

_____

Genesis 29:28 Did Jacob marry Rachel?

_____ Yes   _____ No

Genesis 29:29 WHO was Rachel's maid?

_____

Genesis 29:30-31 HOW does Jacob feel about Leah and Rachel?

_____

Isn't that sad? Have you ever felt like you were unloved?

_____

Tell WHY or WHY not on the lines below.

_____

_____

Genesis 29:31 WHAT do you see about the Lord?

_____

WHAT did the Lord do for Leah?

_____

Isn't that awesome? God is loving and compassionate. God sees everything that happens to us. He saw that Leah was unloved, and He shows her His incredible love for her. He opens her womb. The womb is where God puts the baby inside the mother. God lets Leah get pregnant.

Did you know that God is the One who gives babies? Do you remember when God closed all the wombs of Abimelech's household because he had taken Sarah, Abraham's wife, in Genesis 20:17-18?

Look up and read Psalm 139:13-16.

> Psalm 139:13 WHO forms us and weaves us in our mother's womb? WHO is this "you"? If you don't know, look back at Psalm 139:1.

_____

Look up and read 1 Samuel 1:5. WHAT did the Lord do to Hannah?

_____

Look up and read 1 Samuel 2:6. WHAT do we see about the Lord?

The Lord _____ and makes _____.

God is sovereign. He is the One who is in control of all our circumstances. When we have a problem, we need to run to Him. God is the One who opens and closes wombs. He alone is the Giver of life.

Go back to Genesis 29:31. WHAT do we see about Rachel?

_____

Genesis 29:32 To WHOM does Leah give birth, and WHY did she name him this name?

_____—"because the _____ has seen my

_____; surely now my husband will

_____ me."

Genesis 29:33 WHO is Leah's second son, and WHY does she name him this name?

_____—"because the Lord has _____ that I

am _____."

Genesis 29:34 WHO is Leah's third son, and WHY does she name him this name?

_____—"now this time my _____ will

become _____ to me."

Genesis 29:35 WHO is Leah's fourth son, and WHY does she name him this name?

_____—"this time I will _____ the

_____."

   Isn't God an awesome God? Did you notice how Leah starts off naming her sons names that show her hurt and distress?

WHO is her focus on: her husband or God?

_____

Now look at what happens when she has Judah.

Is there a change in her focus and attitude? _____

WHO is her focus on now? _____

WHERE should our focus be when things are hard and difficult: on our circumstances or on our God who is in control of all our circumstances?

_____

Just like Leah praised the Lord when she had Judah, we need to remember to praise God, even when things are hard and difficult. 1 Thessalonians 5:18 says, "In everything give thanks; for this is God's will for you in Christ Jesus."

We can thank God even in hard times, because we know that God loves us and will work all things—even bad things—for our good (Romans 8:28).

Now let's turn to the family tree on page 31 and add Jacob's wives' and children's names to his side of the family tree.

Way to go! Don't give up!

Day Five

SiSTERS iN CONFLiCT

"Whoa," Lauren called out as she began sliding down the trail.

"Be careful," George warned. "It's still a little slippery on this part of the trail."

"Will we make it back to our main campsite today?" Molly asked. "I'm ready for the bathhouse."

Mr. Burt laughed. "We should make it before nightfall. Are you tired of roughing it out in the middle of the forest?"

About that time, Sam took off barking through the forest. "Oh no!" Max called to his dad. "What set him off this time?"

Mr. Burt laughed at Max's exasperation with Sam. "Hey, Max, he's the great detective beagle. He can't help it. There are so many cool things for him to investigate in the forest. I'm sure he'll come back in a few minutes."

Five minutes down the trail, Molly started sniffing and looked at Lauren. "Do you smell that horrible smell?"

"I sure do. Do you smell it, Dad?"

Mr. Paul looked at Mr. Burt, as Mr. Luke shook his head. Mr. Luke looked over at Max. "Max, I think the great detective beagle has discovered a skunk. Yep, here he comes."

"Oh no," Molly and Lauren squealed. "Get away, Sam! Don't come over here. Yuck. You stink!"

Mr. Burt laughed. "Sam, old boy, as soon as we hit the clearing, you are going to take a tomato-juice bath so we can stand the rest of our adventure."

Finally we made it to the clearing. Let's pull out our maps to find out what is going on with Rachel and Leah, while Sam gets a tomato-juice bath to take away his stink.

Let's pray. Then we are ready to read our maps. Today we are going to read only part of Genesis 30. Read Genesis 30:1-24 and mark the following key words for these verses:

God (Lord) (draw a purple triangle and color it yellow)

Jacob (circle it in blue)

Rachel (color it pink)

Leah (box it in green and color it green)

Underline each child's name and what his name means in blue. Then write the mother's name next to her son's in the margin.

Now, let's find out what is happening with these two sisters.

Genesis 30:1 WHAT is Rachel feeling in this verse?

_____

WHY does she feel this way?

_____

WHOM does Rachel ask for children?

_____

Can he give them to her? _____ Yes   _____ No

WHO is in control? WHO gives children?

_____

Genesis 30:2 HOW does Jacob feel?

_____

Does Jacob know WHO is the giver of children?

_____

Genesis 30:3 WHAT is Rachel's solution to her problem?

_____

Have we seen this happen before? HOW about with Sarah and Hagar?

WHAT should Rachel do instead of trying to get her own way?

_____

Genesis 30:5-6 WHOM does Bilhah give birth to, and WHY does Rachel give him this name?

_____—"_____ has _____ me

and has indeed _____ my voice."

Genesis 30:7-8 WHOM does Bilhah give birth to, and WHY does Rachel give him this name?

_____—"With mighty wrestlings I have

_____ with my _____, and I have

indeed _____."

Genesis 30:9 WHAT did Leah do when she stopped having children?

_____

Genesis 30:10-11 WHOM does Zilpah give birth, to and WHY does Leah give him this name?

_____—"How _____."

Genesis 30:12-13 WHOM does Zilpah give birth to, and WHY does Leah give him this name?

_____—"_____ am I! For women will call

me _____."

Genesis 30:14-15 WHAT is happening with Leah and Rachel in these verses?

_____

_____

(By the way, a mandrake is a small yellow berry.)

Genesis 30:16 WHAT did Leah tell Jacob when he came in from the field?

_____

WHAT is going on with these sisters? Are they competing for Jacob and children? Is this the way sisters should treat each other?

Genesis 30:17-18 WHOM does Leah give birth to, and WHY does she give him this name?

_____—"_____ has given me my

_____."

Genesis 30:19-29 WHOM does Leah give birth to, and WHY does she give him this name?

_____—"_____ has endowed me with a

_____ _____."

Genesis 30:21 WHOM does Leah give birth to?

_____

Genesis 30:22 WHAT happens to Rachel?

_____

Genesis 30:23-24 WHOM does Rachel give birth to, and WHY does she give him this name?

_____—"May the _____ give me another

_____."

Looking at Joseph's name (it means "God will add"), was Rachel satisfied after God remembered her?

_____

Do you ever act like that? Are you grateful for what you have, or do you want more than you have been given?

Write out your answer on the line below.

_____

HOW should you respond to what you have, whether it is a little or a lot?

_____

Now turn to page 31 and add all of Jacob's children's names under their mothers' names on the family tree.
Way to go! Don't forget to say your memory verse to a grown-up!

4

JACOB WRESTLES WITH GOD

GENESIS 30-36

You did it! You made it back to the main campsite. Did you get a good night's sleep after we finally got Sam to quit smelling so bad? We have had an awesome adventure so far. Let's eat our pancakes and find out what's next.

Day
One

GOD BLESSES JACOB

"Hey, guys," Georgiana called out as she walked up to the campsite. "Mr. Burt asked that I come by and see if you are ready for the next part of your great adventure."

"We sure are," Max answered. "How about Sam? Are we taking him?"

"Not this time. We're going to leave Sam with Mr. Burt's wife, Roxanne. She will make sure he stays out of trouble while we take you guys out to ride mountain bikes."

117

"All right! That is so cool," Alex cried out. "I have always wanted to learn how to do some off-road riding. I'm sorry you can't go, Sam, but this is going to be great fun."

How about you? Have you ever done any mountain bike riding? Let's go drop Sam off with Roxanne and pick out our mountain bikes. But before we do, Mr. Burt wants us to look over the trail.

So pull out those maps, and let's get started. Don't forget to pray. Last week we read Genesis 30:1-24 and watched God give Jacob eleven sons and one daughter as part of His plan for this adventurer's life.

Today let's head back to Genesis 30 and work on the rest of this chapter. Let's read Genesis 30:25-43 and mark the following key words for these verses:

God (Lord) (draw a purple triangle and color it yellow)

Jacob (circle it in blue)

Rachel (color it pink)

bless (blessed) (draw a blue cloud and color it pink)

Don't forget to mark anything that tells you WHERE by double-underlining the WHERE in green. And don't forget to mark anything that tells you WHEN by drawing a green clock like this:

Now let's find out what happens after Rachel gives birth to Joseph.

Genesis 30:25–26 WHAT does Jacob ask Laban?

_____

Genesis 30: 27 WHY doesn't Laban want Jacob to leave?

_____

Genesis 30:30 Did Laban have a little or a lot before Jacob came?

_____

WHAT does Jacob want to do?

_____ for his own household

Genesis 30:31-32 WHAT does Jacob want as his wage for staying and keeping Laban's flocks?

_____

Genesis 30:34 Does Laban agree?

_____

Genesis 30:37-38 WHAT did Jacob do when the flocks came to drink?_____

_____

Genesis 30:39 WHAT kinds of babies did they have? Draw a picture below of what the babies looked like.

Genesis 30:42 WHOSE flock was stronger?

_____

Genesis 30:43 WHAT do we see about Jacob?

_____

All right! Tomorrow we will learn how Laban's family feels about all that God has given to Jacob. Now that we are ready to ride, let's discover this week's memory verse.

Look at the bike's tires below. Follow the letters around the tires. Begin at the start position. Cross out every third letter. Go from the outer rim towards the hub, following the arrows. When you finish with the front tire, continue on the rear tire. Put the letters that remain on the blanks below to spell out your verse.

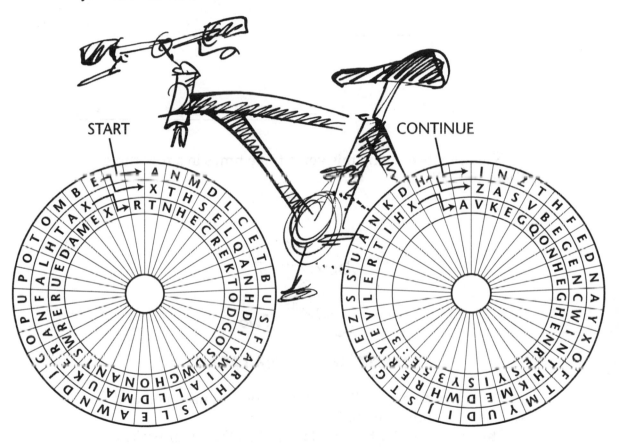

" ___ ___ ___ __ _____ ___

__ __ __ _____, ___

— ___ ____ __ _____

_____ __ ___, ___

_____ _ __ __ ___

___ __ __ _____

__ ___ ____ ____ __

_____ _ ____

___."

                    _____ __:_

Now practice saying this verse three times in a row three times today!

Day
Two

jacob Flees From Laban

"Watch out," Max called out as he picked up speed and started descending the hill.

"Keep your weight back, Max, and feather your brakes," George called out. "Now you've got the feel of it." As Max met up with George and the others at the bottom of the hill, she asked, "Are you ready to try the bunny hop?"

"Yeah, that sounds like fun."

"Okay, as we pedal along, I want each of you to look for a place you want to jump. Before you get there, bend down over your bike like this, with your weight low. Then when you're ready to jump, spring your body up and lift up the handlebars at the same time. As soon as the front wheel starts to lift, pull your legs and feet so that the rear wheel lifts as well. When you come down, relax your arms and legs and allow them to absorb the shock of your landing. Then try to level out your bike so that both wheels land at the same time. Okay, now you give it a try. But remember, this takes lots of practice."

That was a lot of fun! Now that we have practiced and learned how to "bunny hop," let's take some time to check our maps. We need to find out what is happening with Jacob and Laban. Let's read Genesis 31 on page 186 and mark the following key words:

God (Lord) (draw a purple triangle and color it yellow)

Jacob (circle it in blue)

Rachel (color it pink)

dream (draw a blue cloud)

angel (draw blue wings and color them yellow)

deceived (box it and color it brown)

covenant (box it in yellow and color it red)

Mizpah (color it orange)

bless (blessed) (draw a blue cloud and color it pink)

Don't forget to mark anything that tells you WHERE by double-underlining the WHERE in green. And don't forget to mark anything that tells you WHEN by drawing a green clock like this:

Now, follow the trail. Ask the 5 W's and an H.

Genesis 31:1-2 WHAT did Jacob see?

_____

Genesis 31:3 WHY does Jacob decide to leave?

_____

Genesis 31:7 HOW had Laban treated Jacob?

_____

Genesis 31:7-9 WHO protected Jacob from Laban and gave him his wealth?

_____

Genesis 31:10-12 HOW did Jacob know about the striped, speckled, and mottled goats?

_____

_____

Genesis 31:13 WHAT does God remind Jacob about?

_____

WHAT does God tell Jacob to do?

_____

Genesis 31:18 WHERE is Jacob headed?

_____

Genesis 31:19 WHAT does Rachel do?

_____

Genesis 31:20 WHAT does Jacob do to Laban?

_____

HOW?

_____

Genesis 31:22–23 WHAT does Laban do when he discovers that Jacob has fled?

_____

Genesis 31:24 WHAT does God do?

_____

WHOM is God protecting?

_____

Genesis 31:26-28 Is Laban happy when he catches up to

Jacob? _____

Genesis 31:29 WHAT do you think he would like to do to Jacob when he catches up with him?

_____

Can he harm Jacob? WHY or WHY not?

_____

Isn't this awesome? No one can touch us if God says no! Jacob deceived Laban by not telling him he was fleeing. Even when we mess up and do the wrong thing, God still loves us and protects us from harm.

Genesis 31:30 WHAT does Laban think Jacob stole?

_____

Did Jacob do this? _____ WHO did? _____

Genesis 31:33-35 Does she confess, or does she lie?

_____

Genesis 31:36 HOW does Jacob respond?

_____

Genesis 31:38-41 HOW long had Jacob served Laban?

_____ years

Genesis 31:41 Has Laban been fair to Jacob? WHAT did he do?

_____

Genesis 31:42 Since Laban had not treated Jacob well, WHAT is the reason Jacob was not sent away empty-handed?

_____

Genesis 31:44 WHAT do Jacob and Laban make?

_____

Do you remember what a covenant is? A covenant is a solemn, binding agreement made by passing through pieces of flesh. It is a treaty, an alliance, a pledge, or an agreement. A covenant is a promise that can never be broken.

Genesis 31:49 The word *Mizpah* means "the watchtower." WHY did Laban call the witness Mizpah?

_____

Genesis 31:52 WHAT did the heap and pillar witness?

_____

Genesis 31:53 WHO is going to judge between them?

_____

Genesis 31:54 WHAT does Jacob do?

_____

Genesis 31:55 WHAT does Laban do early the next morning?

_____

Wow! Just look at how God has kept His promises. God has been with Jacob these 20 years, blessing him and Laban. He does not allow Laban to do harm to Jacob, and He brings about a peaceful departure between Jacob and Laban.

God is also bringing Jacob back to the land of promise. God is a faithful and good God. Even though Jacob has made many mistakes, God still loves him and will bring about His plan and His purpose for Jacob's life. Do you know that God loves you and will do the very same thing for you, if you just put your faith and trust in Him?

Now don't forget to practice your memory verse! Then head back on the trail with your mountain bike. You are looking really good!

Day Three

WRESTLING WITH GOD

"Hey, Sam, old boy, did you have a good time with Mrs. Roxanne?" Max petted Sam and gave him a doggie treat. "Thanks, Mrs. Roxanne, for watching Sam. We had an awesome time on our mountain bikes."

"I'm glad you did, Max," replied Roxanne. "Has Mr. Burt told you about taking the leap of faith today?"

"No. What's the leap of faith?"

Roxanne just smiled. "You'll see. I'm going to come out and watch. You will probably love it. Have fun, and I'll see you in a little while."

So are you ready to take the leap of faith? It's a very exciting adventure that requires your trust as you leap out in midair to try and catch a trapeze hanging from a pole about 20 feet off the ground. Let's go meet the others and get ready for some scary fun!

But before we step out in faith, we need to

spend some time on God's extreme adventure. Jacob and Laban have just cut a covenant and parted ways. Jacob is on his way back to the land of Canaan. Do you remember why Jacob left the land? WHO wanted to kill Jacob for stealing his blessing? _____ How do you think Jacob feels as he heads back home? Let's find out. Talk to your Expert Guide and then turn to page 191.

Read Genesis chapters 32–33 and mark the following key words in both chapters of Scripture:

God (Lord) (draw a purple triangle and color it yellow)

Jacob (circle it in blue)

Esau (color it red)

angel (draw blue wings and color them yellow)

pray (draw a purple ⌂ and color it pink)

bless (blessed) (draw a blue cloud and color it pink)

Rachel (color it pink)

Leah (box it in green and color it green)

altar (box it in red)

Don't forget to mark anything that tells you WHERE by double-underlining the <u>WHERE</u> in green. And don't forget to mark anything that tells you WHEN by drawing a green clock like this: 🕒

Now ask the 5 W's and an H.

Genesis 32:1 WHOM does Jacob meet as he goes on his way?

The _____ of God

Genesis 32:3 To WHOM did Jacob send messengers?

His brother _____

Genesis 32:5 WHAT is Jacob hoping will happen?

That he will find _____ in Esau's sight

Remember, the last time Jacob saw Esau was 20 years ago and Esau wanted to kill him.

Genesis 32:6 HOW many men does the messenger tell Jacob are coming with Esau?

_____ _____ men
(circle both these words together in
the word search)

Genesis 32:7 HOW does Jacob feel?

He was greatly _____ and

_____.

Uh-oh. How would you feel if you knew your brother wanted to kill you, and you hear he is on his way with 400 men?

Genesis 32:7 WHAT does Jacob do?

He divides the people into _____ _____.

Genesis 32:8 WHY does he do this?

If Esau a ___ ___ ___ ___ ___s one company, then the

company that is left will _____.

Genesis 32:9-12 WHAT does Jacob do?

Genesis 32:11 He p __ __ __ s to the

Lord and asks God to _____

him from the hand of his brother.

The first time that Jacob is afraid of Esau, he runs away. But this time, instead of running away, he turns to God and asks God to deliver him.

He reminds God of His promises and prays God's Word back to Him! Look at how Jacob has changed.

Genesis 32:13 WHAT does Jacob select for his brother?

A _____

Genesis 32:20 WHAT is Jacob hoping this present will do?

A ___ ___ ___ __ __ e Esau so he will _____
Jacob

Even though Jacob is trusting God, we see that he is still worried about seeing his brother. Have you ever worried over something that might or might not happen in your life?

_____ Yes   _____ No

WHAT was it?

_____

_____

Should you worry, since you know that God is a good God who loves you and promises that everything that comes into your life, even if it is hard, will work together for good?

_____

WHAT will you do the next time you start to worry?

_____

Genesis 32:24 WHAT happens to Jacob that night after he sends his wives, maids, and children ahead of him, and he is left alone?

A _____ _____ with him until daybreak.

Genesis 32:25 WHAT happens when the man does not

prevail against Jacob? He _____ the socket of

Jacob's _____ and _____ it.

Genesis 32:26 WHAT did Jacob want the man to do

before he lets him go? _____ him

Genesis 32:28 WHAT happened?

He changed Jacob's _____ to _____.

WHY did he do this?

Because Jacob has _____ with _____ and
prevailed

Genesis 32:28,30 WHO was the man Jacob was wrestling

with? WHOM did Jacob see face-to-face? _____

Amazing! The name *Jacob* means "one who takes by the heel or supplants." Now Jacob's name has been changed to *Israel*, which means "he who strives with God" or "God strives."

Isn't it awesome to see how God changes Jacob's name to show the change in his life? Jacob has been struggling all of his life. First, Jacob struggles in the womb with Esau. Then he struggles with Esau over the birthright and over the stolen blessing. Jacob struggled with Laban over his two daughters, while he had to deal with his wives' conflict over him and having children. He struggles with Laban over his possessions, and now here he is wrestling with God.

Jacob has been wrestling against God all of his life. As Jacob meets God face-to-face, he hangs on to God and is changed. Jacob finally submits to God.

Through all these struggles, we have seen Jacob make many mistakes, but he never gave up or quit. He held on to God.

HOW about you? Are you wrestling with God over the control of your life, or have you met Him face-to-face and surrendered your life to Him?

_____

Will you give up when the going gets tough, or will you hang on and persevere until the end?

_____

Genesis 32:31 WHAT do we see that is different about Jacob as he crosses over Penuel?

He was _____ on his thigh.

Genesis 33:1 WHOM does Jacob see coming?

_____

The moment of truth has arrived. Does it say anywhere in this chapter (Genesis 33) that Jacob is afraid?

_____

No! Now that Jacob has been face-to-face with God, there is no mention of fear. Being in God's presence changes us. Do you spend time with God every day?

_____

Genesis 33:4 WHAT happens when Jacob finally meets Esau?

Esau ran to meet him and _____ him and

_____him, and they _____.

Isn't that amazing? Not only has Jacob changed, but Esau has changed, too! At some point—either in the 20 years Jacob was gone, or after Esau heads out with his 400 men, and Jacob prays and asks God to deliver him—there is a change in Esau's heart. Awesome! God can change our circumstances and our hearts, and take away our fear. When something hard or difficult happens, we need to run to God and get our strength from Him.

Genesis 33:6-7 WHAT do the wives and children do

when they meet Esau? They _____ down.

Genesis 33:11 WHAT does Jacob want to give Esau?

His _____ because God has dealt graciously with

him and given him plenty

Genesis 33:12 WHAT does Esau offer to do?

To _____ before Jacob

Genesis 33:14 WHAT is Jacob's response?

"Please let my lord _____ on before his servant,

and I will _____ at my leisure."

Genesis 33:16 WHAT does Esau do?

He _____ that day on his way to _____.

Genesis 33:20 WHAT did Jacob do after he arrived in
Shechem and bought land?

He erected an _____ and called it El-Elohe-

Israel.

This name *El-Elohe-Israel* means "God, the God of Israel." Before this time, Jacob has always called God the God of Abraham and Isaac. Now after Jacob's struggle is finally over, we see Jacob calling God his God, the God of Israel.

God has kept Jacob on his journey and brought him safely home. He is a faithful God who has kept His promises!

Now go back to pages 132-138 and find all the answers that you filled in the blanks from both passages of Scripture in the word search below. If an answer is used more than one time, you only need to find it once.

D	I	S	L	O	C	A	T	E	D	E	S	S	I	K
E	S	A	U	Q	E	S	A	E	P	P	A	S	L	T
R	E	M	B	R	A	C	E	D	C	S	E	E	E	B
D	E	S	S	E	R	T	S	I	D	K	S	L	A	S
N	F	S	S	A	P	D	O	D	N	C	C	B	R	E
U	S	N	T	Q	S	E	E	C	P	A	A	D	S	L
H	Y	L	R	S	D	L	Z	R	A	T	P	P	I	P
R	A	D	I	U	I	T	E	C	N	T	E	M	R	R
U	R	I	V	V	T	S	C	G	Z	A	P	J	O	O
O	P	A	E	I	E	E	M	A	N	I	M	D	V	C
F	M	R	N	P	R	R	P	N	A	E	W	A	E
G	N	F	T	T	W	W	R	G	P	W	Z	H	F	E
H	Q	A	F	H	G	I	H	T	O	U	C	H	E	D
S	J	C	I	W	E	P	T	B	W	D	O	M	P	O
Y	Q	O	G	S	N	D	O	V	T	F	O	I	I	Y

Fantastic! You did it! Now check your harness, climb up on the pole, and jump off with a leap of faith.

Day Four

JACOB WORSHIPS GOD

Now that you made the leap of faith, let's head over to the triple zip line for a 750-foot wild ride down the side of the mountain and across the water. Doesn't that sound like fun? Grab your maps and swimsuits, and let's head up to the top of the zip line.

"Hey, Max," Molly called out, "I'll time you and Alex as you go down the zip line. Then you can time Lauren and me to see who goes the fastest."

"That's a great idea. Look at that. Did you just see that boy flip around and around on the water? This is going to be one wild, wet ride."

"Come on, Max," Alex called out. "It's our turn. 'Bye, girls. See you in the water."

"One, two, three, we're off. Yee-ha!" Max yelled as he, Alex, and Mr. Paul went flying down the mountain and skimmed across the river.

Wahoooooo o oo o oo ooo!

"That was awesome!" Max laughed at the end of the course. "Let's sit over here and time Molly and Lauren."

Max, Molly, and the others continued to ride the zip line until Mr. Burt called for a lunch break. Let's eat. Then we need to pull out our maps and find out what's happening on Jacob's adventure now that he is back in the land of Canaan. Don't forget to pray! Then turn to page 198.

Read Genesis 35 and mark the following key words:

God (Lord) (draw a purple triangle and color it yellow)

Jacob (circle it in blue)

Esau (color it red)

altar (box it in red)

died (draw a black tombstone and color it brown)

bless (blessed) (draw a blue cloud and color it pink)

Rachel (color it pink)

Leah (box it in green and color it green)

Don't forget to mark anything that tells you WHERE by double-underlining the WHERE in green. And don't forget to mark anything that tells you WHEN by drawing a green clock like this:

Now ask the 5 W's and an H.

Genesis 35:1 WHAT does God tell Jacob to do?

_____

In Genesis we have seen men building altars to God but this is the first time that God asks someone to build an altar to Him.

Genesis 35:2 WHAT does Jacob tell his household to do?

_____

_____

WHY do you think Jacob tells them to do these things?

_____

_____

Could it be because Jacob knew not to bring any foreign idols or gods into a holy God's presence? God is a jealous God. We are to love Him with all our heart and soul. We are to be clean when we come into His presence. We are not to worship anyone but Him!

Genesis 35:4 WHAT did Jacob do with the foreign gods?

_____

Genesis 35:6-7 WHERE does Jacob build the altar?

_____

Circle this place in green on the map below.

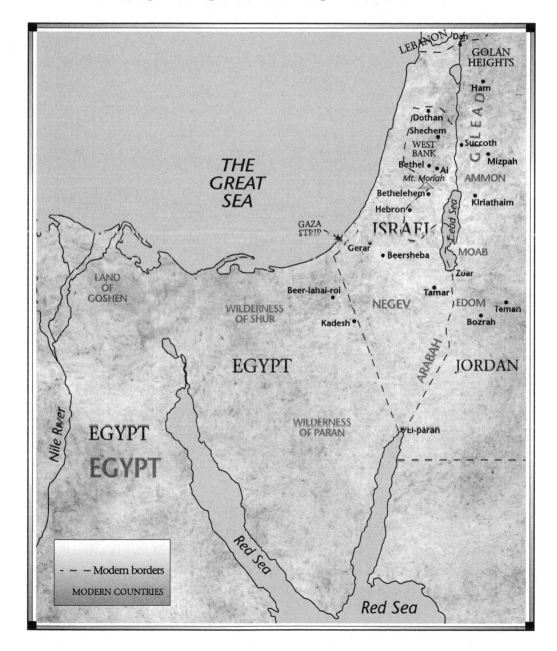

Genesis 35:7 WHAT did Jacob (Israel) call this place?

_____

This name means "the God of the house of God."

Genesis 35:7 WHEN was the first time that God revealed Himself to Jacob at this same place?

_____

Genesis 35:9 WHAT does God do when He appears to Jacob again?

_____

Genesis 35:10 WHAT does God say to Jacob?

_____

Genesis 35:11 WHO does God show Jacob He is?

"I am _____ _____."

The Hebrew name for God Almighty is *El Shaddai* (pronounced el sha-DIE). It means just what it says: God is the almighty One, the powerful or mighty One. God is all-sufficient. He is all that we need. When we are weak, He is strong. He is all-powerful! He can do anything!

Genesis 35:11-12 WHAT does God tell Jacob?

"Be _____ and _____.

A _____ and a company of _____ shall

come from you. And _____ shall come forth from

you. The _____ which I gave to Abraham and Isaac, I

will _____ it to you, and I will give the

_____ to your _____ after you."

Genesis 35:14 WHAT did Jacob do after God spoke with him?

_____

WHAT is this? It's worship. Jacob is worshiping God!

Genesis 35:16-17 WHAT happens to Rachel as they leave Bethel on their journey to Ephrath?

_____

Genesis 35:18 WHAT happens to Rachel?

_____

WHAT does she name this son?

_____

This name means "son of my trouble."

WHAT does Jacob name him instead?

_____

This name means "son of my right hand."

Now turn back to the family tree on page 31 and add this last son of Jacob to the family tree.

Genesis 35:22 HOW many sons did Jacob (Israel) have?

_____ sons

Name them.

_____

_____

Did you know that these 12 sons will become the 12 tribes of Israel?

Genesis 35:28-29 WHAT happens to Isaac?

_____

Genesis 35:28 HOW old was he? _____ years old

Genesis 35:29 WHO buried Isaac?

_____

These two brothers who have always struggled are together to bury their father. What an exciting adventure we have had with Isaac, Jacob, and Esau.

Tomorrow we will take another look at Esau and his family as our extreme adventure with the three guys in God's plan comes to an end. Don't forget to practice your memory verse!

ESAU'S DESCENDANTS

Can you believe this is the last day of our extreme adventure with God? We have had so much fun and made many new friends as we learned about Isaac, Esau, Jacob, God, and His plan.

Since this is our last day, how about one more white-water rafting adventure? Mr. Burt says we can take Sam if we take a calmer ride down the lower Pigeon River. Let's go get our PFDs and helmets and head back to the river.

That was awesome! Did you see Sam when that wave washed over the side? He almost went crazy barking before Max got him to settle down. He is one crazy pup, but he loved his adventure.

Let's head back to our adventure with Jacob and Esau. Now that Jacob and Esau have buried Isaac, let's find out about Esau's family and the nation of Edom. Don't forget to pray. Then turn to page 200. Read Genesis 36 and mark the following key words and key phrase:

Now these are the records of the generations of (circle it in blue)

Jacob (Israel) (circle it in blue)

Esau (Edom) (color it red)

land (that refers to the land of Canaan) (double-underline it in green and color it blue)

Don't forget to mark anything that tells you WHERE by double-underlining the WHERE in green. And don't forget to mark anything that tells you WHEN by drawing a green clock like this: 🕐

Now go back to Isaac's family tree on page 31. Look up the verses of Scripture on the family tree and add the names of Esau's wives and children.

Genesis 36:6-7 WHY did Esau take his family and all his belongings and move away from the land of Canaan?

_____

Genesis 36:9 WHOM is Esau the father of? WHAT are they called?

_____

WHERE do they live?

_____

Now let's find out a little more about Esau's descendants. Let's look at Esau's firstborn son, Eliphaz. Did you notice the name of Eliphaz's son by his concubine Timna (Genesis 36:12)? WHAT is this son's name?

_____

Let's look up some passages to see what we can learn about Amalek. Look up and read Exodus 17:8-16.

Genesis 17:8 WHO came and fought against the nation of Israel?

_____

Genesis 17:16 WHAT did the Lord swear?

_____

Look up and read Deuteronomy 25:17-19.

Deuteronomy 25:17-18 WHAT did Amalek do to the children of Israel as they came out of Egypt?

_____

Deuteronomy 25:19 WHAT are they (the children of Israel) to do when God gives them rest from all their enemies in the land?

_____

Look up and read 1 Samuel 15:1-3.

1 Samuel 15:2 WHY does God want to punish Amalek?

_____

Did you know that Israel's first and constant enemy is Amalek, Esau's grandson? WHY would God want to blot out Amalek? Remember Jacob's blessing in Genesis 27:29: "Cursed be those who curse you, and blessed be those who bless you."

Amalek would not let the nation of Israel pass through the land of Edom. Amalek also came out and fought against Israel at Rephidim. Because Amalek has come against Israel, God's chosen nation, God will blot out the memory of Amalek from under heaven.

Now let's see what else we can discover about Edom. Take a look at Max and Molly's map below to learn a little bit about Esau's nation, the nation of Edom.

EDOM

- If you look on the map on page 143 you will see that Edom lies southeast of the Dead Sea on the opposite side of the Arabah.

- The terrain is made up of red sandstone, and guess what the name Edom means? It means "red" or "ruddy."

- Edom is also a wilderness and does not grow crops very well. Does this remind you of the blessing in Genesis 27:39 when Isaac told Esau that he would live away from the fertility of the earth and the dew of heaven?

- The capital of Edom is Bozrah. The present name is Buseirah.

- Teman is a city located in southern Edom and is associated with an Edomite clan of Teman, who descended from Esau (Genesis 36:10-11).

- Most of Edom today is now a part of the kingdom of Jordan. There is a part of present-day Jordan that is a part of the land promised to Abraham, Isaac, and Jacob, but this part does not include the territory of Moab or Edom.

- Because Esau is Jacob's brother, the Israelites regard the Edomites as close relatives. They are even referred to as "brothers."

Now let's look up a few passages of Scripture about Edom.
Look up and read Joshua 24:3-4

Joshua 24:4 WHAT did God give Esau?

_____

Look up and read Ezekiel 25:12-14.

Ezekiel 25:13 WHAT is God going to do to Edom?

_____

_____

Ezekiel 25:14 WHAT is God going to put on Edom?

_____

This is in the future. It hasn't happened yet.

Look up and read Isaiah 63:1-6.

Isaiah 63:1 WHERE is He coming from?

_____

WHAT will His garments look like?

_____

HOW does He speak?

_____

Isaiah 63:2 WHAT do we see about His apparel?

_____

Isaiah 63:3 WHY are his garments red? WHAT is sprinkled on them?

_____

Isaiah 63:4 WHAT is on His heart?

_____

WHAT is this the year of?

_____

Now compare this Scripture passage in Isaiah to Revelation 19:13-15.

Revelation 19:13 WHAT is His robe dipped in?

_____

WHAT is His name called?

_____

Revelation 19:15 WHAT comes from His mouth, and WHAT will He do with it?

_____

HOW will He rule?

_____

WHAT does He tread?

_____

Do you know WHO this "He" is in Isaiah and Revelation? It's Jesus Christ at His second coming to the earth. Now draw a picture in the box below that describes Jesus in these verses in Isaiah 63.

Let's look at one more passage. Look up and read Joel 3:18-21.

Joel 3:19 WHAT will happen to Edom?

_____

WHY? _____

Joel 3:20 WHAT do we see about Judah and Jerusalem?

_____

Joel 3:21 WHAT will God do?

_____

This will be fulfilled when Jesus returns to earth. There will be no one in Edom because of the violence that was done to Jacob. WHEN did this all begin? WHAT book of the Bible are you studying?

_____

That's right. It all began at the beginning in Genesis, and it has not been completed yet. Will it? WHAT do you think?

WHAT did you learn about God by following our three guys in God's plan? God is faithful. He always keeps His promises! What He says He will do. His name is El Shaddai. He is God Almighty. He is all-powerful. Nothing is too difficult for Him!

As we wrap up our extreme adventure with God, we need to remember all the things that we have learned about God so that when hard times and struggles come, we will run to God and hang on to Him until He gives us the victory in the end!

Don't forget to say your memory verse one more time. Just like God was with Jacob in his day of distress, God will be with you wherever you go.

BACK AT THE CAMPSITE

You did it! You completed your extreme adventure with God. Just look at how much you have grown. You know how to hang tough and persevere to the end.

You have watched Isaac make the same mistakes his father did, and seen Esau sell his birthright for a bowl of stew, and then watched Jacob deceive both his father and brother to make sure he received the blessing. And through all their mistakes, you saw that God is a faithful God who can clean up messes and fulfill His purpose.

God is sovereign. He is in control of our circumstances. He has a perfect plan for each one of us, and no one can thwart His plan or purpose.

You have also seen how important prayer is, and that you need to ask God to guide you each and every day. You saw through prayer how God led and provided Isaac with his wife, Rebekah. You have also seen how much pain that lies and deception can bring. You have watched Jacob wrestle with God and finally surrender.

But most importantly, you learned that you have a birthright if you have accepted Jesus Christ as your Savior. There is a blessing in heaven waiting just for you! One day very soon, Jesus will come back and take us to live with Him in heaven. Now that will be one *extreme* adventure!

You have done an awesome job! We are so proud of you! Don't forget to fill out the card in the back of this book. We want to send you a special certificate for helping us out on *Extreme Adventures with God*. Keep up the good work! Why don't you come with us as we head next to New York City to make a comic book on the life of Jacob's son Joseph—God's superhero! It will be one very exciting adventure! See you in God's Word real soon!

Molly, Max, and

(Sam)

PUZZLE ANSWERS

Page 13

For though the <u>twins</u> were not yet <u>born</u> and had not done anything <u>good</u> or <u>bad</u>, so that <u>God's</u> <u>purpose</u> according to <u>His</u> <u>choice</u> would <u>stand</u>, not because of <u>works</u> but because of <u>Him</u> who <u>calls</u>...

—<u>Romans</u> 9:11

Page 38

Pages 52-53

The <u>Scripture</u>, foreseeing that <u>God</u> would <u>justify</u> the Gentiles by <u>faith</u>, <u>preached</u> the <u>gospel</u> beforehand to <u>Abraham</u>, saying, "All the <u>nations</u> will be <u>blessed</u> in you." So then <u>those</u> who are of <u>faith</u> are <u>blessed</u> with Abraham, the <u>believer</u>.

— <u>Galatians</u> 3:8-9

Page 77

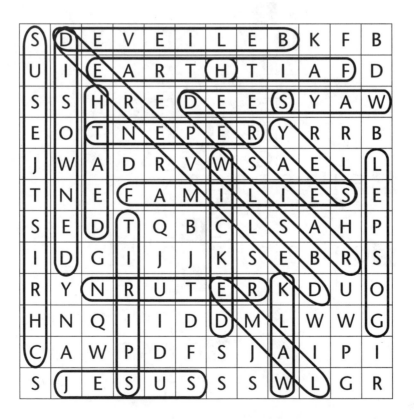

Page 87

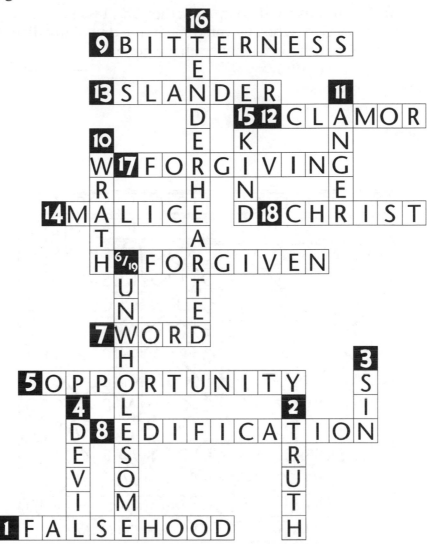

Page 91

Be kind to one another, tender-hearted, forgiving each other, just as God in Christ also has forgiven you.

—Ephesians 4:32

Pages 121-22

"And let us arise and go up to Bethel, and I will make an altar there to God, who answered me in the day of my distress and has been with me wherever I have gone."

—Genesis 35:3

Page 139

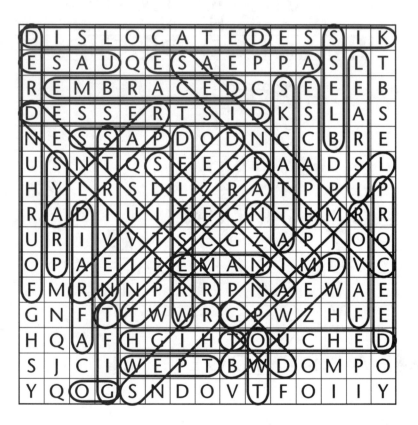

Observation Worksheets

GENESIS 24

1   Now Abraham was old, advanced in age; and the LORD had blessed Abraham in every way.

2   Abraham said to his servant, the oldest of his household, who had charge of all that he owned, "Please place your hand under my thigh,

3   and I will make you swear by the LORD, the God of heaven and the God of earth, that you shall not take a wife for my son from the daughters of the Canaanites, among whom I live,

4   but you will go to my country and to my relatives, and take a wife for my son Isaac."

5   The servant said to him, "Suppose the woman is not willing to follow me to this land; should I take your son back to the land from where you came?"

6   Then Abraham said to him, "Beware that you do not take my son back there!

7   "The LORD, the God of heaven, who took me from my father's house and from the land of my birth, and who spoke to me and who swore to me, saying, 'To your descendants I will give this land,' He will send His angel before you, and you will take a wife for my son from there.

8   "But if the woman is not willing to follow you, then you will be free from this my oath; only do not take my son back there."

9   So the servant placed his hand under the thigh of Abraham his master, and swore to him concerning this matter.

10   Then the servant took ten camels from the camels of his master, and set out with a variety of good things of his master's in his hand; and he arose and went to Mesopotamia, to the city of Nahor.

11   He made the camels kneel down outside the city by the well of water at evening time, the time when women go out to draw water.

12   He said, "O LORD, the God of my master Abraham, please grant me success today, and show lovingkindness to my master Abraham.

13   "Behold, I am standing by the spring, and the daughters of the men of the city are coming out to draw water;

14   now may it be that the girl to whom I say, 'Please let down your jar so that I may drink,' and who answers, 'Drink, and I will water your camels also'—*may* she *be the one* whom You have appointed for Your servant Isaac; and by this I will know that You have shown lovingkindness to my master."

15   Before he had finished speaking, behold, Rebekah who was born to Bethuel the son of Milcah, the wife of Abraham's brother Nahor, came out with her jar on her shoulder.

16   The girl was very beautiful, a virgin, and no man had had relations with her; and she went down to the spring and filled her jar and came up.

17   Then the servant ran to meet her, and said, "Please let me drink a little water from your jar."

18   She said, "Drink, my lord"; and she quickly lowered her jar to her hand, and gave him a drink.

19   Now when she had finished giving him a drink, she said, "I will draw also for your camels until they have finished drinking."

20   So she quickly emptied her jar into the trough, and ran back to the well to draw, and she drew for all his camels.

21   Meanwhile, the man was gazing at her in silence, to know whether the LORD had made his journey successful or not.

22   When the camels had finished drinking, the man took a gold ring weighing a half-shekel and two bracelets for her wrists weighing ten shekels in gold,

23 and said, "Whose daughter are you? Please tell me, is there room for us to lodge in your father's house?"

24 She said to him, "I am the daughter of Bethuel, the son of Milcah, whom she bore to Nahor."

25 Again she said to him, "We have plenty of both straw and feed, and room to lodge in."

26 Then the man bowed low and worshiped the LORD.

27 He said, "Blessed be the LORD, the God of my master Abraham, who has not forsaken His lovingkindness and His truth toward my master; as for me, the LORD has guided me in the way to the house of my master's brothers."

28 Then the girl ran and told her mother's household about these things.

29 Now Rebekah had a brother whose name was Laban; and Laban ran outside to the man at the spring.

30 When he saw the ring and the bracelets on his sister's wrists, and when he heard the words of Rebekah his sister, saying, "This is what the man said to me," he went to the man; and behold, he was standing by the camels at the spring.

31 And he said, "Come in, blessed of the LORD! Why do you stand outside since I have prepared the house, and a place for the camels?"

32 So the man entered the house. Then Laban unloaded the camels, and he gave straw and feed to the camels, and water to wash his feet and the feet of the men who were with him.

33 But when *food* was set before him to eat, he said, "I will not eat until I have told my business." And he said, "Speak on."

34 So he said, "I am Abraham's servant.

35 "The LORD has greatly blessed my master, so that he has become rich; and He has given him flocks and herds, and silver and gold, and servants and maids, and camels and donkeys.

36 "Now Sarah my master's wife bore a son to my master in her old age, and he has given him all that he has.

37 "My master made me swear, saying, 'You shall not take a wife for my son from the daughters of the Canaanites, in whose land I live;

38 but you shall go to my father's house and to my relatives, and take a wife for my son.'

39 "I said to my master, 'Suppose the woman does not follow me.'

40 "He said to me, 'The LORD, before whom I have walked, will send His angel with you to make your journey successful, and you will take a wife for my son from my relatives and from my father's house;

41 then you will be free from my oath, when you come to my relatives; and if they do not give her to you, you will be free from my oath.'

42 "So I came today to the spring, and said, 'O LORD, the God of my master Abraham, if now You will make my journey on which I go successful;

43 behold, I am standing by the spring, and may it be that the maiden who comes out to draw, and to whom I say, "Please let me drink a little water from your jar";

44 and she will say to me, "You drink, and I will draw for your camels also"; let her be the woman whom the LORD has appointed for my master's son.'

45 "Before I had finished speaking in my heart, behold, Rebekah came out with her jar on her shoulder, and went down to the spring and drew, and I said to her, 'Please let me drink.'

46 "She quickly lowered her jar from her *shoulder,* and said, 'Drink, and I will water your camels also'; so I drank, and she watered the camels also.

47 "Then I asked her, and said, 'Whose daughter are you?' And she said, 'The daughter of Bethuel, Nahor's son, whom Milcah bore to him'; and I put the ring on her nose, and the bracelets on her wrists.

48 "And I bowed low and worshiped the LORD, and blessed the LORD, the God of my master Abraham, who had guided me in the right way to take the daughter of my master's kinsman for his son.

49 "So now if you are going to deal kindly and truly with my master, tell me; and if not, let me know, that I may turn to the right hand or the left."

50 Then Laban and Bethuel replied, "The matter comes from the LORD; *so* we cannot speak to you bad or good.

51 "Here is Rebekah before you, take *her* and go, and let her be the wife of your master's son, as the LORD has spoken."

52 When Abraham's servant heard their words, he bowed himself to the ground before the LORD.

53 The servant brought out articles of silver and articles of gold, and garments, and gave them to Rebekah; he also gave precious things to her brother and to her mother.

54 Then he and the men who were with him ate and drank and spent the night. When they arose in the morning, he said, "Send me away to my master."

55 But her brother and her mother said, "Let the girl stay with us *a few* days, say ten; afterward she may go."

56 He said to them, "Do not delay me, since the LORD has prospered my way. Send me away that I may go to my master."

57 And they said, "We will call the girl and consult her wishes."

58 Then they called Rebekah and said to her, "Will you go with this man?" And she said, "I will go."

59 Thus they sent away their sister Rebekah and her nurse with Abraham's servant and his men.

60 They blessed Rebekah and said to her,

"May you, our sister,

Become thousands of ten thousands,

And may your descendants possess

The gate of those who hate them."

61 Then Rebekah arose with her maids, and they mounted the camels and followed the man. So the servant took Rebekah and departed.

62 Now Isaac had come from going to Beer-lahai-roi; for he was living in the Negev.

63 Isaac went out to meditate in the field toward evening; and he lifted up his eyes and looked, and behold, camels were coming.

64 Rebekah lifted up her eyes, and when she saw Isaac she dismounted from the camel.

65 She said to the servant, "Who is that man walking in the field to meet us?" And the servant said, "He is my master." Then she took her veil and covered herself.

66 The servant told Isaac all the things that he had done.

67 Then Isaac brought her into his mother Sarah's tent, and he took Rebekah, and she became his wife, and he loved her; thus Isaac was comforted after his mother's death.

GENESIS 25

1 Now Abraham took another wife, whose name was Keturah.

2 She bore to him Zimran and Jokshan and Medan and Midian and Ishbak and Shuah.

3 Jokshan became the father of Sheba and Dedan. And the sons of Dedan were Asshurim and Letushim and Leummim.

4 The sons of Midian *were* Ephah and Epher and Hanoch and Abida and Eldaah. All these *were* the sons of Keturah.

5   Now Abraham gave all that he had to Isaac;

6   but to the sons of his concubines, Abraham gave gifts while he was still living, and sent them away from his son Isaac eastward, to the land of the east.

7   These are all the years of Abraham's life that he lived, one hundred and seventy-five years.

8   Abraham breathed his last and died in a ripe old age, an old man and satisfied *with life;* and he was gathered to his people.

9   Then his sons Isaac and Ishmael buried him in the cave of Machpelah, in the field of Ephron the son of Zohar the Hittite, facing Mamre,

10 the field which Abraham purchased from the sons of Heth; there Abraham was buried with Sarah his wife.

11 It came about after the death of Abraham, that God blessed his son Isaac; and Isaac lived by Beer-lahai-roi.

12 Now these are the records of the generations of Ishmael, Abraham's son, whom Hagar the Egyptian, Sarah's maid, bore to Abraham;

13 and these are the names of the sons of Ishmael, by their names, in the order of their birth: Nebaioth, the firstborn of Ishmael, and Kedar and Adbeel and Mibsam

14 and Mishma and Dumah and Massa,

15 Hadad and Tema, Jetur, Naphish and Kedemah.

16 These are the sons of Ishmael and these are their names, by their villages, and by their camps; twelve princes according to their tribes.

17 These are the years of the life of Ishmael, one hundred and thirty-seven years; and he breathed his last and died, and was gathered to his people.

18 They settled from Havilah to Shur which is east of Egypt as one goes toward Assyria; he settled in defiance of all his relatives.

19 Now these are the records of the generations of Isaac, Abraham's son: Abraham became the father of Isaac;

20 and Isaac was forty years old when he took Rebekah, the daughter of Bethuel the Aramean of Paddan-aram, the sister of Laban the Aramean, to be his wife.

21 Isaac prayed to the LORD on behalf of his wife, because she was barren; and the LORD answered him and Rebekah his wife conceived.

22 But the children struggled together within her; and she said, "If it is so, why then am I *this way?*" So she went to inquire of the LORD.

23 The LORD said to her,

"Two nations are in your womb;

And two peoples will be separated from your body;

And one people shall be stronger than the other;

And the older shall serve the younger."

24 When her days to be delivered were fulfilled, behold, there were twins in her womb.

25 Now the first came forth red, all over like a hairy garment; and they named him Esau.

26 Afterward his brother came forth with his hand holding on to Esau's heel, so his name was called Jacob; and Isaac was sixty years old when she gave birth to them.

27 When the boys grew up, Esau became a skillful hunter, a man of the field, but Jacob was a peaceful man, living in tents.

28 Now Isaac loved Esau, because he had a taste for game, but Rebekah loved Jacob.

29 When Jacob had cooked stew, Esau came in from the field and he was famished;

30 and Esau said to Jacob, "Please let me have a swallow of that red stuff there, for I am famished." Therefore his name was called Edom.

31 But Jacob said, "First sell me your birthright."

32 Esau said, "Behold, I am about to die; so of what *use* then is the birthright to me?"

33 And Jacob said, "First swear to me"; so he swore to him, and sold his birthright to Jacob.

34 Then Jacob gave Esau bread and lentil stew; and he ate and drank, and rose and went on his way. Thus Esau despised his birthright.

GENESIS 26

1 Now there was a famine in the land, besides the previous famine that had occurred in the days of Abraham. So Isaac went to Gerar, to Abimelech king of the Philistines.

2 The LORD appeared to him and said, "Do not go down to Egypt; stay in the land of which I shall tell you.

3 "Sojourn in this land and I will be with you and bless you, for to you and to your descendants I will give all these lands, and I will establish the oath which I swore to your father Abraham.

4 "I will multiply your descendants as the stars of heaven, and will give your descendants all these lands; and by your descendants all the nations of the earth shall be blessed;

5 because Abraham obeyed Me and kept My charge, My commandments, My statutes and My laws."

6 So Isaac lived in Gerar.

7 When the men of the place asked about his wife, he said, "She is my sister," for he was afraid to say, "my wife," *thinking*, "the men of the place might kill me on account of Rebekah, for she is beautiful."

8 It came about, when he had been there a long time, that Abimelech king of the Philistines looked out through a window, and saw, and behold, Isaac was caressing his wife Rebekah.

9   Then Abimelech called Isaac and said, "Behold, certainly she is your wife! How then did you say, 'She is my sister'?" And Isaac said to him, "Because I said, 'I might die on account of her.'"

10   Abimelech said, "What is this you have done to us? One of the people might easily have lain with your wife, and you would have brought guilt upon us."

11   So Abimelech charged all the people, saying, "He who touches this man or his wife shall surely be put to death."

12   Now Isaac sowed in that land and reaped in the same year a hundredfold. And the LORD blessed him,

13   and the man became rich, and continued to grow richer until he became very wealthy;

14   for he had possessions of flocks and herds and a great household, so that the Philistines envied him.

15   Now all the wells which his father's servants had dug in the days of Abraham his father, the Philistines stopped up by filling them with earth.

16   Then Abimelech said to Isaac, "Go away from us, for you are too powerful for us."

17   And Isaac departed from there and camped in the valley of Gerar, and settled there.

18   Then Isaac dug again the wells of water which had been dug in the days of his father Abraham, for the Philistines had stopped them up after the death of Abraham; and he gave them the same names which his father had given them.

19   But when Isaac's servants dug in the valley and found there a well of flowing water,

20   the herdsmen of Gerar quarreled with the herdsmen of Isaac, saying, "The water is ours!" So he named the well Esek, because they contended with him.

21 Then they dug another well, and they quarreled over it too, so he named it Sitnah.

22 He moved away from there and dug another well, and they did not quarrel over it; so he named it Rehoboth, for he said, "At last the LORD has made room for us, and we will be fruitful in the land."

23 Then he went up from there to Beersheba.

24 The LORD appeared to him the same night and said,

> "I am the God of your father Abraham;
>
> Do not fear, for I am with you.
>
> I will bless you, and multiply your descendants,
>
> For the sake of My servant Abraham."

25 So he built an altar there and called upon the name of the LORD, and pitched his tent there; and there Isaac's servants dug a well.

26 Then Abimelech came to him from Gerar with his adviser Ahuzzath and Phicol the commander of his army.

27 Isaac said to them, "Why have you come to me, since you hate me and have sent me away from you?"

28 They said, "We see plainly that the LORD has been with you; so we said, 'Let there now be an oath between us, *even* between you and us, and let us make a covenant with you,

29 that you will do us no harm, just as we have not touched you and have done to you nothing but good and have sent you away in peace. You are now the blessed of the LORD.'"

30 Then he made them a feast, and they ate and drank.

31 In the morning they arose early and exchanged oaths; then Isaac sent them away and they departed from him in peace.

32 Now it came about on the same day, that Isaac's servants came in and told him about the well which they had dug, and said to him, "We have found water."

33 So he called it Shibah; therefore the name of the city is Beersheba to this day.

34 When Esau was forty years old he married Judith the daughter of Beeri the Hittite, and Basemath the daughter of Elon the Hittite;

35 and they brought grief to Isaac and Rebekah.

CHAPTER 27

1 Now it came about, when Isaac was old and his eyes were too dim to see, that he called his older son Esau and said to him, "My son." And he said to him, "Here I am."

2 Isaac said, "Behold now, I am old *and* I do not know the day of my death.

3 "Now then, please take your gear, your quiver and your bow, and go out to the field and hunt game for me;

4 and prepare a savory dish for me such as I love, and bring it to me that I may eat, so that my soul may bless you before I die."

5 Rebekah was listening while Isaac spoke to his son Esau. So when Esau went to the field to hunt for game to bring *home*,

6 Rebekah said to her son Jacob, "Behold, I heard your father speak to your brother Esau, saying,

7 'Bring me *some* game and prepare a savory dish for me, that I may eat, and bless you in the presence of the LORD before my death.'

8 "Now therefore, my son, listen to me as I command you.

9 "Go now to the flock and bring me two choice young goats from there, that I may prepare them *as* a savory dish for your father, such as he loves.

10 "Then you shall bring *it* to your father, that he may eat, so that he may bless you before his death."

11 Jacob answered his mother Rebekah, "Behold, Esau my brother is a hairy man and I am a smooth man.

12 "Perhaps my father will feel me, then I will be as a deceiver in his sight, and I will bring upon myself a curse and not a blessing."

13 But his mother said to him, "Your curse be on me, my son; only obey my voice, and go, get *them* for me."

14 So he went and got *them,* and brought *them* to his mother; and his mother made savory food such as his father loved.

15 Then Rebekah took the best garments of Esau her elder son, which were with her in the house, and put them on Jacob her younger son.

16 And she put the skins of the young goats on his hands and on the smooth part of his neck.

17 She also gave the savory food and the bread, which she had made, to her son Jacob

18 Then he came to his father and said, "My father." And he said, "Here I am. Who are you, my son?"

19 Jacob said to his father, "I am Esau your firstborn; I have done as you told me. Get up, please, sit and eat of my game, that you may bless me."

20 Isaac said to his son, "How is it that you have *it* so quickly, my son?" And he said, "Because the LORD your God caused *it* to happen to me."

21 Then Isaac said to Jacob, "Please come close, that I may feel you, my son, whether you are really my son Esau or not."

22 So Jacob came close to Isaac his father, and he felt him and said, "The voice is the voice of Jacob, but the hands are the hands of Esau."

23 He did not recognize him, because his hands were hairy like his brother Esau's hands; so he blessed him.

24 And he said, "Are you really my son Esau?" And he said, "I am."

25 So he said, "Bring *it* to me, and I will eat of my son's game, that I may bless you." And he brought *it* to him, and he ate; he also brought him wine and he drank.

26 Then his father Isaac said to him, "Please come close and kiss me, my son."

27 So he came close and kissed him; and when he smelled the smell of his garments, he blessed him and said,

"See, the smell of my son

Is like the smell of a field which the LORD has blessed;

28 Now may God give you of the dew of heaven,

And of the fatness of the earth,

And an abundance of grain and new wine;

29 May peoples serve you,

And nations bow down to you;

Be master of your brothers,

And may your mother's sons bow down to you.

Cursed be those who curse you,

And blessed be those who bless you."

30 Now it came about, as soon as Isaac had finished blessing Jacob, and Jacob had hardly gone out from the presence of Isaac his father, that Esau his brother came in from his hunting.

31 Then he also made savory food, and brought it to his father; and he said to his father, "Let my father arise and eat of his son's game, that you may bless me."

32 Isaac his father said to him, "Who are you?" And he said, "I am your son, your firstborn, Esau."

33 Then Isaac trembled violently, and said, "Who was he then that hunted game and brought *it* to me, so that I ate of all *of it* before you came, and blessed him? Yes, and he shall be blessed."

34 When Esau heard the words of his father, he cried out with an exceedingly great and bitter cry, and said to his father, "Bless me, *even* me also, O my father!"

35 And he said, "Your brother came deceitfully and has taken away your blessing."

36 Then he said, "Is he not rightly named Jacob, for he has supplanted me these two times? He took away my birthright, and behold, now he has taken away my blessing." And he said, "Have you not reserved a blessing for me?"

37 But Isaac replied to Esau, "Behold, I have made him your master, and all his relatives I have given to him as servants; and with grain and new wine I have sustained him. Now as for you then, what can I do, my son?"

38 Esau said to his father, "Do you have only one blessing, my father? Bless me, *even* me also, O my father." So Esau lifted his voice and wept.

39 Then Isaac his father answered and said to him,

"Behold, away from the fertility of the earth shall be your dwelling,

And away from the dew of heaven from above.

40 "By your sword you shall live,

And your brother you shall serve;

But it shall come about when you become restless,

That you will break his yoke from your neck."

41 So Esau bore a grudge against Jacob because of the blessing with which his father had blessed him; and Esau said to himself, "The days of mourning for my father are near; then I will kill my brother Jacob."

42 Now when the words of her elder son Esau were reported to Rebekah, she sent and called her younger son Jacob, and said to him, "Behold your brother Esau is consoling himself concerning you *by planning* to kill you.

43 "Now therefore, my son, obey my voice, and arise, flee to Haran, to my brother Laban!

44 "Stay with him a few days, until your brother's fury subsides,

45 until your brother's anger against you subsides and he forgets what you did to him. Then I will send and get you from there. Why should I be bereaved of you both in one day?"

46 Rebekah said to Isaac, "I am tired of living because of the daughters of Heth; if Jacob takes a wife from the daughters of Heth, like these, from the daughters of the land, what good will my life be to me?"

CHAPTER 28

1 So Isaac called Jacob and blessed him and charged him, and said to him, "You shall not take a wife from the daughters of Canaan.

2 "Arise, go to Paddan-aram, to the house of Bethuel your mother's father; and from there take to yourself a wife from the daughters of Laban your mother's brother.

3 "May God Almighty bless you and make you fruitful and multiply you, that you may become a company of peoples.

4 "May He also give you the blessing of Abraham, to you and to your descendants with you, that you may possess the land of your sojournings, which God gave to Abraham."

5 Then Isaac sent Jacob away, and he went to Paddan-aram to Laban, son of Bethuel the Aramean, the brother of Rebekah, the mother of Jacob and Esau.

6 Now Esau saw that Isaac had blessed Jacob and sent him away to Paddan-aram to take to himself a wife from there, *and that* when he blessed him he charged him, saying, "You shall not take a wife from the daughters of Canaan,"

7   and that Jacob had obeyed his father and his mother and had gone to Paddan-aram.

8   So Esau saw that the daughters of Canaan displeased his father Isaac;

9   and Esau went to Ishmael, and married, besides the wives that he had, Mahalath the daughter of Ishmael, Abraham's son, the sister of Nebaioth.

10 Then Jacob departed from Beersheba and went toward Haran.

11 He came to a certain place and spent the night there, because the sun had set; and he took one of the stones of the place and put it under his head, and lay down in that place.

12 He had a dream, and behold, a ladder was set on the earth with its top reaching to heaven; and behold, the angels of God were ascending and descending on it.

13 And behold, the LORD stood above it and said, "I am the LORD, the God of your father Abraham and the God of Isaac; the land on which you lie, I will give it to you and to your descendants.

14 "Your descendants will also be like the dust of the earth, and you will spread out to the west and to the east and to the north and to the south; and in you and in your descendants shall all the families of the earth be blessed.

15 "Behold, I am with you and will keep you wherever you go, and will bring you back to this land; for I will not leave you until I have done what I have promised you."

16 Then Jacob awoke from his sleep and said, "Surely the LORD is in this place, and I did not know it."

17 He was afraid and said, "How awesome is this place! This is none other than the house of God, and this is the gate of heaven."

18 So Jacob rose early in the morning, and took the stone that he had put under his head and set it up as a pillar and poured oil on its top.

19 He called the name of that place Bethel; however, previously the name of the city had been Luz.

20 Then Jacob made a vow, saying, "If God will be with me and will keep me on this journey that I take, and will give me food to eat and garments to wear,

21 and I return to my father's house in safety, then the LORD will be my God.

22 "This stone, which I have set up as a pillar, will be God's house, and of all that You give me I will surely give a tenth to You."

CHAPTER 29

1 Then Jacob went on his journey, and came to the land of the sons of the east.

2 He looked, and saw a well in the field, and behold, three flocks of sheep were lying there beside it, for from that well they watered the flocks. Now the stone on the mouth of the well was large.

3 When all the flocks were gathered there, they would then roll the stone from the mouth of the well and water the sheep, and put the stone back in its place on the mouth of the well.

4 Jacob said to them, "My brothers, where are you from?" And they said, "We are from Haran."

5 He said to them, "Do you know Laban the son of Nahor?" And they said, "We know *him*."

6 And he said to them, "Is it well with him?" And they said, "It is well, and here is Rachel his daughter coming with the sheep."

7 He said, "Behold, it is still high day; it is not time for the livestock to be gathered. Water the sheep, and go, pasture them."

8 But they said, "We cannot, until all the flocks are gathered, and they roll the stone from the mouth of the well; then we water the sheep."

9 While he was still speaking with them, Rachel came with her father's sheep, for she was a shepherdess.

10 When Jacob saw Rachel the daughter of Laban his mother's brother, and the sheep of Laban his mother's brother, Jacob went up and rolled the stone from the mouth of the well and watered the flock of Laban his mother's brother.

11 Then Jacob kissed Rachel, and lifted his voice and wept.

12 Jacob told Rachel that he was a relative of her father and that he was Rebekah's son, and she ran and told her father.

13 So when Laban heard the news of Jacob his sister's son, he ran to meet him, and embraced him and kissed him and brought him to his house. Then he related to Laban all these things.

14 Laban said to him, "Surely you are my bone and my flesh." And he stayed with him a month.

15 Then Laban said to Jacob, "Because you are my relative, should you therefore serve me for nothing? Tell me, what shall your wages be?"

16 Now Laban had two daughters; the name of the older was Leah, and the name of the younger was Rachel.

17 And Leah's eyes were weak, but Rachel was beautiful of form and face.

18 Now Jacob loved Rachel, so he said, "I will serve you seven years for your younger daughter Rachel."

19 Laban said, "It is better that I give her to you than to give her to another man; stay with me."

20 So Jacob served seven years for Rachel and they seemed to him but a few days because of his love for her.

21   Then Jacob said to Laban, "Give *me* my wife, for my time is completed, that I may go in to her."

22   Laban gathered all the men of the place and made a feast.

23   Now in the evening he took his daughter Leah, and brought her to him; and *Jacob* went in to her.

24   Laban also gave his maid Zilpah to his daughter Leah as a maid.

25   So it came about in the morning that, behold, it was Leah! And he said to Laban, "What is this you have done to me? Was it not for Rachel that I served with you? Why then have you deceived me?"

26   But Laban said, "It is not the practice in our place to marry off the younger before the firstborn.

27   "Complete the week of this one, and we will give you the other also for the service which you shall serve with me for another seven years."

28   Jacob did so and completed her week, and he gave him his daughter Rachel as his wife.

29   Laban also gave his maid Bilhah to his daughter Rachel as her maid.

30   So *Jacob* went in to Rachel also, and indeed he loved Rachel more than Leah, and he served with Laban for another seven years.

31   Now the LORD saw that Leah was unloved, and He opened her womb, but Rachel was barren.

32   Leah conceived and bore a son and named him Reuben, for she said, "Because the LORD has seen my affliction; surely now my husband will love me."

33   Then she conceived again and bore a son and said, "Because the LORD has heard that I am unloved, He has therefore given me this *son* also." So she named him Simeon.

34 She conceived again and bore a son and said, "Now this time my husband will become attached to me, because I have borne him three sons." Therefore he was named Levi.

35 And she conceived again and bore a son and said, "This time I will praise the LORD." Therefore she named him Judah. Then she stopped bearing.

CHAPTER 30

1 Now when Rachel saw that she bore Jacob no children, she became jealous of her sister; and she said to Jacob, "Give me children, or else I die."

2 Then Jacob's anger burned against Rachel, and he said, "Am I in the place of God, who has withheld from you the fruit of the womb?"

3 She said, "Here is my maid Bilhah, go in to her that she may bear on my knees, that through her I too may have children."

4 So she gave him her maid Bilhah as a wife, and Jacob went in to her.

5 Bilhah conceived and bore Jacob a son.

6 Then Rachel said, "God has vindicated me, and has indeed heard my voice and has given me a son." Therefore she named him Dan.

7 Rachel's maid Bilhah conceived again and bore Jacob a second son.

8 So Rachel said, "With mighty wrestlings I have wrestled with my sister, *and* I have indeed prevailed." And she named him Naphtali.

9 When Leah saw that she had stopped bearing, she took her maid Zilpah and gave her to Jacob as a wife.

10 Leah's maid Zilpah bore Jacob a son.

11 Then Leah said, "How fortunate!" So she named him Gad.

12 Leah's maid Zilpah bore Jacob a second son.

13 Then Leah said, "Happy am I! For women will call me happy." So she named him Asher.

14 Now in the days of wheat harvest Reuben went and found mandrakes in the field, and brought them to his mother Leah. Then Rachel said to Leah, "Please give me some of your son's mandrakes."

15 But she said to her, "Is it a small matter for you to take my husband? And would you take my son's mandrakes also?" So Rachel said, "Therefore he may lie with you tonight in return for your son's mandrakes."

16 When Jacob came in from the field in the evening, then Leah went out to meet him and said, "You must come in to me, for I have surely hired you with my son's mandrakes." So he lay with her that night.

17 God gave heed to Leah, and she conceived and bore Jacob a fifth son.

18 Then Leah said, "God has given me my wages because I gave my maid to my husband." So she named him Issachar.

19 Leah conceived again and bore a sixth son to Jacob.

20 Then Leah said, "God has endowed me with a good gift; now my husband will dwell with me, because I have borne him six sons." So she named him Zebulun.

21 Afterward she bore a daughter and named her Dinah.

22 Then God remembered Rachel, and God gave heed to her and opened her womb.

23 So she conceived and bore a son and said, "God has taken away my reproach."

24 She named him Joseph, saying, "May the LORD give me another son."

25 Now it came about when Rachel had borne Joseph, that Jacob said to Laban, "Send me away, that I may go to my own place and to my own country.

26 "Give *me* my wives and my children for whom I have served you, and let me depart; for you yourself know my service which I have rendered you."

27 But Laban said to him, "If now it pleases you, *stay with me;* I have divined that the LORD has blessed me on your account."

28 He continued, "Name me your wages, and I will give it."

29 But he said to him, "You yourself know how I have served you and how your cattle have fared with me.

30 "For you had little before I came and it has increased to a multitude, and the LORD has blessed you wherever I turned. But now, when shall I provide for my own household also?"

31 So he said, "What shall I give you?" And Jacob said, "You shall not give me anything. If you will do this *one* thing for me, I will again pasture *and* keep your flock:

32 let me pass through your entire flock today, removing from there every speckled and spotted sheep and every black one among the lambs and the spotted and speckled among the goats; and *such* shall be my wages.

33 "So my honesty will answer for me later, when you come concerning my wages. Every one that is not speckled and spotted among the goats and black among the lambs, *if found* with me, will be considered stolen."

34 Laban said, "Good, let it be according to your word."

35 So he removed on that day the striped and spotted male goats and all the speckled and spotted female goats, every one with white in it, and all the black ones among the sheep, and gave them into the care of his sons.

36 And he put *a distance of* three days' journey between himself and Jacob, and Jacob fed the rest of Laban's flocks.

37 Then Jacob took fresh rods of poplar and almond and plane trees, and peeled white stripes in them, exposing the white which *was* in the rods.

38 He set the rods which he had peeled in front of the flocks in the gutters, *even* in the watering troughs, where the flocks came to drink; and they mated when they came to drink.

39 So the flocks mated by the rods, and the flocks brought forth striped, speckled, and spotted.

40 Jacob separated the lambs, and made the flocks face toward the striped and all the black in the flock of Laban; and he put his own herds apart, and did not put them with Laban's flock.

41 Moreover, whenever the stronger of the flock were mating, Jacob would place the rods in the sight of the flock in the gutters, so that they might mate by the rods;

42 but when the flock was feeble, he did not put *them* in; so the feebler were Laban's and the stronger Jacob's.

43 So the man became exceedingly prosperous, and had large flocks and female and male servants and camels and donkeys.

CHAPTER 31

1 Now Jacob heard the words of Laban's sons, saying, "Jacob has taken away all that was our father's, and from what belonged to our father he has made all this wealth."

2 Jacob saw the attitude of Laban, and behold, it was not *friendly* toward him as formerly.

3 Then the LORD said to Jacob, "Return to the land of your fathers and to your relatives, and I will be with you."

4 So Jacob sent and called Rachel and Leah to his flock in the field,

5 and said to them, "I see your father's attitude, that it is not *friendly* toward me as formerly, but the God of my father has been with me.

6 "You know that I have served your father with all my strength.

7 "Yet your father has cheated me and changed my wages ten times; however, God did not allow him to hurt me.

8 "If he spoke thus, 'The speckled shall be your wages,' then all the flock brought forth speckled; and if he spoke thus, 'The striped shall be your wages,' then all the flock brought forth striped.

9 "Thus God has taken away your father's livestock and given *them* to me.

10 "And it came about at the time when the flock were mating that I lifted up my eyes and saw in a dream, and behold, the male goats which were mating *were* striped, speckled, and mottled.

11 "Then the angel of God said to me in the dream, 'Jacob,' and I said, 'Here I am.'

12 "He said, 'Lift up now your eyes and see *that* all the male goats which are mating are striped, speckled, and mottled; for I have seen all that Laban has been doing to you.

13 'I am the God *of* Bethel, where you anointed a pillar, where you made a vow to Me; now arise, leave this land, and return to the land of your birth.'"

14 Rachel and Leah said to him, "Do we still have any portion or inheritance in our father's house?

15 "Are we not reckoned by him as foreigners? For he has sold us, and has also entirely consumed our purchase price.

16 "Surely all the wealth which God has taken away from our father belongs to us and our children; now then, do whatever God has said to you."

17 Then Jacob arose and put his children and his wives upon camels;

18 and he drove away all his livestock and all his property which he had gathered, his acquired livestock which he had gathered in Paddan-aram, to go to the land of Canaan to his father Isaac.

19 When Laban had gone to shear his flock, then Rachel stole the household idols that were her father's.

20 And Jacob deceived Laban the Aramean by not telling him that he was fleeing.

21 So he fled with all that he had; and he arose and crossed the *Euphrates* River, and set his face toward the hill country of Gilead.

22 When it was told Laban on the third day that Jacob had fled,

23 then he took his kinsmen with him and pursued him *a distance of* seven days' journey, and he overtook him in the hill country of Gilead.

24 God came to Laban the Aramean in a dream of the night and said to him, "Be careful that you do not speak to Jacob either good or bad."

25 Laban caught up with Jacob. Now Jacob had pitched his tent in the hill country, and Laban with his kinsmen camped in the hill country of Gilead.

26 Then Laban said to Jacob, "What have you done by deceiving me and carrying away my daughters like captives of the sword?

27 "Why did you flee secretly and deceive me, and did not tell me so that I might have sent you away with joy and with songs, with timbrel and with lyre;

28 and did not allow me to kiss my sons and my daughters? Now you have done foolishly.

29 "It is in my power to do you harm, but the God of your father spoke to me last night, saying, 'Be careful not to speak either good or bad to Jacob.'

30 "Now you have indeed gone away because you longed greatly for your father's house; *but* why did you steal my gods?"

31 Then Jacob replied to Laban, "Because I was afraid, for I thought that you would take your daughters from me by force.

32 "The one with whom you find your gods shall not live; in the presence of our kinsmen point out what is yours among my belongings and take *it* for yourself." For Jacob did not know that Rachel had stolen them.

33 So Laban went into Jacob's tent and into Leah's tent and into the tent of the two maids, but he did not find *them*. Then he went out of Leah's tent and entered Rachel's tent.

34 Now Rachel had taken the household idols and put them in the camel's saddle, and she sat on them. And Laban felt through all the tent but did not find *them*.

35 She said to her father, "Let not my lord be angry that I cannot rise before you, for the manner of women is upon me." So he searched but did not find the household idols.

36 Then Jacob became angry and contended with Laban; and Jacob said to Laban, "What is my transgression? What is my sin that you have hotly pursued me?

37 "Though you have felt through all my goods, what have you found of all your household goods? Set *it* here before my kinsmen and your kinsmen, that they may decide between us two.

38 "These twenty years I *have been* with you; your ewes and your female goats have not miscarried, nor have I eaten the rams of your flocks.

39 "That which was torn *of beasts* I did not bring to you; I bore the loss of it myself. You required it of my hand *whether* stolen by day or stolen by night.

40 "*Thus* I was: by day the heat consumed me and the frost by night, and my sleep fled from my eyes.

41 "These twenty years I have been in your house; I served you fourteen years for your two daughters and six years for your flock, and you changed my wages ten times.

42 "If the God of my father, the God of Abraham, and the fear of Isaac, had not been for me, surely now you would have sent me away empty-handed. God has seen my affliction and the toil of my hands, so He rendered judgment last night."

43 Then Laban replied to Jacob, "The daughters are my daughters, and the children are my children, and the flocks are my flocks, and all that you see is mine. But what can I do this day to these my daughters or to their children whom they have borne?

44 "So now come, let us make a covenant, you and I, and let it be a witness between you and me."

45 Then Jacob took a stone and set it up *as* a pillar.

46 Jacob said to his kinsmen, "Gather stones." So they took stones and made a heap, and they ate there by the heap.

47 Now Laban called it Jegar-sahadutha, but Jacob called it Galeed.

48 Laban said, "This heap is a witness between you and me this day." Therefore it was named Galeed,

49 and Mizpah, for he said, "May the LORD watch between you and me when we are absent one from the other.

50 "If you mistreat my daughters, or if you take wives besides my daughters, *although* no man is with us, see, God is witness between you and me."

51 Laban said to Jacob, "Behold this heap and behold the pillar which I have set between you and me.

52 "This heap is a witness, and the pillar is a witness, that I will not pass by this heap to you for harm, and you will not pass by this heap and this pillar to me, for harm.

53 "The God of Abraham and the God of Nahor, the God of their father, judge between us." So Jacob swore by the fear of his father Isaac.

54 Then Jacob offered a sacrifice on the mountain, and called his kinsmen to the meal; and they ate the meal and spent the night on the mountain.

55 Early in the morning Laban arose, and kissed his sons and his daughters and blessed them. Then Laban departed and returned to his place.

CHAPTER 32

1   Now as Jacob went on his way, the angels of God met him.

2   Jacob said when he saw them, "This is God's camp." So he named that place Mahanaim.

3   Then Jacob sent messengers before him to his brother Esau in the land of Seir, the country of Edom.

4   He also commanded them saying, "Thus you shall say to my lord Esau: 'Thus says your servant Jacob, "I have sojourned with Laban, and stayed until now;

5   I have oxen and donkeys *and* flocks and male and female servants; and I have sent to tell my lord, that I may find favor in your sight."'"

6   The messengers returned to Jacob, saying, "We came to your brother Esau, and furthermore he is coming to meet you, and four hundred men are with him."

7   Then Jacob was greatly afraid and distressed; and he divided the people who were with him, and the flocks and the herds and the camels, into two companies;

8   for he said, "If Esau comes to the one company and attacks it, then the company which is left will escape."

9 Jacob said, "O God of my father Abraham and God of my father Isaac, O LORD, who said to me, 'Return to your country and to your relatives, and I will prosper you,'

10 I am unworthy of all the lovingkindness and of all the faithfulness which You have shown to Your servant; for with my staff *only* I crossed this Jordan, and now I have become two companies.

11 "Deliver me, I pray, from the hand of my brother, from the hand of Esau; for I fear him, that he will come and attack me *and* the mothers with the children.

12 "For You said, 'I will surely prosper you and make your descendants as the sand of the sea, which is too great to be numbered.'"

13 So he spent the night there. Then he selected from what he had with him a present for his brother Esau:

14 two hundred female goats and twenty male goats, two hundred ewes and twenty rams,

15 thirty milking camels and their colts, forty cows and ten bulls, twenty female donkeys and ten male donkeys.

16 He delivered *them* into the hand of his servants, every drove by itself, and said to his servants, "Pass on before me, and put a space between droves."

17 He commanded the one in front, saying, "When my brother Esau meets you and asks you, saying, 'To whom do you belong, and where are you going, and to whom do these *animals* in front of you belong?'

18 then you shall say, '*These* belong to your servant Jacob; it is a present sent to my lord Esau. And behold, he also is behind us.'"

19 Then he commanded also the second and the third, and all those who followed the droves, saying, "After this manner you shall speak to Esau when you find him;

20 and you shall say, 'Behold, your servant Jacob also is behind us.'" For he said, "I will appease him with the present that goes before me. Then afterward I will see his face; perhaps he will accept me."

21 So the present passed on before him, while he himself spent that night in the camp.

22 Now he arose that same night and took his two wives and his two maids and his eleven children, and crossed the ford of the Jabbok.

23 He took them and sent them across the stream. And he sent across whatever he had.

24 Then Jacob was left alone, and a man wrestled with him until daybreak.

25 When he saw that he had not prevailed against him, he touched the socket of his thigh; so the socket of Jacob's thigh was dislocated while he wrestled with him.

26 Then he said, "Let me go, for the dawn is breaking." But he said, "I will not let you go unless you bless me."

27 So he said to him, "What is your name?" And he said, "Jacob."

28 He said, "Your name shall no longer be Jacob, but Israel; for you have striven with God and with men and have prevailed."

29 Then Jacob asked him and said, "Please tell me your name." But he said, "Why is it that you ask my name?" And he blessed him there.

30 So Jacob named the place Peniel, for *he said*, "I have seen God face to face, yet my life has been preserved."

31 Now the sun rose upon him just as he crossed over Penuel, and he was limping on his thigh.

32 Therefore, to this day the sons of Israel do not eat the sinew of the hip which is on the socket of the thigh, because he touched the socket of Jacob's thigh in the sinew of the hip.

CHAPTER 33

1 Then Jacob lifted his eyes and looked, and behold, Esau was coming, and four hundred men with him. So he divided the children among Leah and Rachel and the two maids.

2 He put the maids and their children in front, and Leah and her children next, and Rachel and Joseph last.

3 But he himself passed on ahead of them and bowed down to the ground seven times, until he came near to his brother.

4 Then Esau ran to meet him and embraced him, and fell on his neck and kissed him, and they wept.

5 He lifted his eyes and saw the women and the children, and said, "Who are these with you?" So he said, "The children whom God has graciously given your servant."

6 Then the maids came near with their children, and they bowed down.

7 Leah likewise came near with her children, and they bowed down; and afterward Joseph came near with Rachel, and they bowed down.

8 And he said, "What do you mean by all this company which I have met?" And he said, "To find favor in the sight of my lord."

9 But Esau said, "I have plenty, my brother; let what you have be your own."

10 Jacob said, "No, please, if now I have found favor in your sight, then take my present from my hand, for I see your face as one sees the face of God, and you have received me favorably.

11 "Please take my gift which has been brought to you, because God has dealt graciously with me and because I have plenty." Thus he urged him and he took *it*.

12 Then Esau said, "Let us take our journey and go, and I will go before you."

13 But he said to him, "My lord knows that the children are frail and that the flocks and herds which are nursing are a care to me. And if they are driven hard one day, all the flocks will die.

14 "Please let my lord pass on before his servant, and I will proceed at my leisure, according to the pace of the cattle that are before me and according to the pace of the children, until I come to my lord at Seir."

15 Esau said, "Please let me leave with you some of the people who are with me." But he said, "What need is there? Let me find favor in the sight of my lord."

16 So Esau returned that day on his way to Seir.

17 Jacob journeyed to Succoth, and built for himself a house and made booths for his livestock; therefore the place is named Succoth.

18 Now Jacob came safely to the city of Shechem, which is in the land of Canaan, when he came from Paddan-aram, and camped before the city.

19 He bought the piece of land where he had pitched his tent from the hand of the sons of Hamor, Shechem's father, for one hundred pieces of money.

20 Then he erected there an altar and called it El-Elohe-Israel.

CHAPTER 34

1   Now Dinah the daughter of Leah, whom she had borne to Jacob, went out to visit the daughters of the land.

2   When Shechem the son of Hamor the Hivite, the prince of the land, saw her, he took her and lay with her by force.

3   He was deeply attracted to Dinah the daughter of Jacob, and he loved the girl and spoke tenderly to her.

4   So Shechem spoke to his father Hamor, saying, "Get me this young girl for a wife."

5   Now Jacob heard that he had defiled Dinah his daughter; but his sons were with his livestock in the field, so Jacob kept silent until they came in.

6   Then Hamor the father of Shechem went out to Jacob to speak with him.

7   Now the sons of Jacob came in from the field when they heard *it;* and the men were grieved, and they were very angry because he had done a disgraceful thing in Israel by lying with Jacob's daughter, for such a thing ought not to be done.

8   But Hamor spoke with them, saying, "The soul of my son Shechem longs for your daughter; please give her to him in marriage.

9   "Intermarry with us; give your daughters to us and take our daughters for yourselves.

10   "Thus you shall live with us, and the land shall be *open* before you; live and trade in it and acquire property in it."

11   Shechem also said to her father and to her brothers, "If I find favor in your sight, then I will give whatever you say to me.

12   "Ask me ever so much bridal payment and gift, and I will give according as you say to me; but give me the girl in marriage."

13   But Jacob's sons answered Shechem and his father Hamor with deceit, because he had defiled Dinah their sister.

14   They said to them, "We cannot do this thing, to give our sister to one who is uncircumcised, for that would be a disgrace to us.

15   "Only on this *condition* will we consent to you: if you will become like us, in that every male of you be circumcised,

16   then we will give our daughters to you, and we will take your daughters for ourselves, and we will live with you and become one people.

17   "But if you will not listen to us to be circumcised, then we will take our daughter and go."

18 Now their words seemed reasonable to Hamor and Shechem, Hamor's son.

19 The young man did not delay to do the thing, because he was delighted with Jacob's daughter. Now he was more respected than all the household of his father.

20 So Hamor and his son Shechem came to the gate of their city and spoke to the men of their city, saying,

21 "These men are friendly with us; therefore let them live in the land and trade in it, for behold, the land is large enough for them. Let us take their daughters in marriage, and give our daughters to them.

22 "Only on this *condition* will the men consent to us to live with us, to become one people: that every male among us be circumcised as they are circumcised.

23 "Will not their livestock and their property and all their animals be ours? Only let us consent to them, and they will live with us."

24 All who went out of the gate of his city listened to Hamor and to his son Shechem, and every male was circumcised, all who went out of the gate of his city.

25 Now it came about on the third day, when they were in pain, that two of Jacob's sons, Simeon and Levi, Dinah's brothers, each took his sword and came upon the city unawares, and killed every male.

26 They killed Hamor and his son Shechem with the edge of the sword, and took Dinah from Shechem's house, and went forth.

27 Jacob's sons came upon the slain and looted the city, because they had defiled their sister.

28 They took their flocks and their herds and their donkeys, and that which was in the city and that which was in the field;

29 and they captured and looted all their wealth and all their little ones and their wives, even all that *was* in the houses.

30 Then Jacob said to Simeon and Levi, "You have brought trouble on me by making me odious among the inhabitants of the land, among the Canaanites and the Perizzites; and my men being few in number, they will gather together against me and attack me and I will be destroyed, I and my household."

31 But they said, "Should he treat our sister as a harlot?"

CHAPTER 35

1 Then God said to Jacob, "Arise, go up to Bethel and live there, and make an altar there to God, who appeared to you when you fled from your brother Esau."

2 So Jacob said to his household and to all who were with him, "Put away the foreign gods which are among you, and purify yourselves and change your garments;

3 and let us arise and go up to Bethel, and I will make an altar there to God, who answered me in the day of my distress and has been with me wherever I have gone."

4 So they gave to Jacob all the foreign gods which they had and the rings which were in their ears, and Jacob hid them under the oak which was near Shechem.

5 As they journeyed, there was a great terror upon the cities which were around them, and they did not pursue the sons of Jacob.

6 So Jacob came to Luz (that is, Bethel), which is in the land of Canaan, he and all the people who were with him.

7 He built an altar there, and called the place El-bethel, because there God had revealed Himself to him when he fled from his brother.

8 Now Deborah, Rebekah's nurse, died, and she was buried below Bethel under the oak; it was named Allon-bacuth.

9 Then God appeared to Jacob again when he came from Paddan-aram, and He blessed him.

10 God said to him,

"Your name is Jacob;

You shall no longer be called Jacob,

But Israel shall be your name."

Thus He called him Israel.

11 God also said to him,

"I am God Almighty;

Be fruitful and multiply;

A nation and a company of nations shall come from you,

And kings shall come forth from you.

12 "The land which I gave to Abraham and Isaac,

I will give it to you,

And I will give the land to your descendants after you."

13 Then God went up from him in the place where He had spoken with him.

14 Jacob set up a pillar in the place where He had spoken with him, a pillar of stone, and he poured out a drink offering on it; he also poured oil on it.

15 So Jacob named the place where God had spoken with him, Bethel.

16 Then they journeyed from Bethel; and when there was still some distance to go to Ephrath, Rachel began to give birth and she suffered severe labor.

17 When she was in severe labor the midwife said to her, "Do not fear, for now you have another son."

18 It came about as her soul was departing (for she died), that she named him Ben-oni; but his father called him Benjamin.

19 So Rachel died and was buried on the way to Ephrath (that is, Bethlehem).

20 Jacob set up a pillar over her grave; that is the pillar of Rachel's grave to this day.

21 Then Israel journeyed on and pitched his tent beyond the tower of Eder.

22 It came about while Israel was dwelling in that land, that Reuben went and lay with Bilhah his father's concubine, and Israel heard *of it*. Now there were twelve sons of Jacob—

23 the sons of Leah: Reuben, Jacob's firstborn, then Simeon and Levi and Judah and Issachar and Zebulun;

24 the sons of Rachel: Joseph and Benjamin;

25 and the sons of Bilhah, Rachel's maid: Dan and Naphtali;

26 and the sons of Zilpah, Leah's maid: Gad and Asher. These are the sons of Jacob who were born to him in Paddan-aram.

27 Jacob came to his father Isaac at Mamre of Kiriath-arba (that is, Hebron), where Abraham and Isaac had sojourned.

28 Now the days of Isaac were one hundred and eighty years.

29 Isaac breathed his last and died and was gathered to his people, an old man of ripe age; and his sons Esau and Jacob buried him.

CHAPTER 36

1 Now these are *the records of* the generations of Esau (that is, Edom).

2 Esau took his wives from the daughters of Canaan: Adah the daughter of Elon the Hittite, and Oholibamah the daughter of Anah and the granddaughter of Zibeon the Hivite;

3 also Basemath, Ishmael's daughter, the sister of Nebaioth.

4 Adah bore Eliphaz to Esau, and Basemath bore Reuel,

5 and Oholibamah bore Jeush and Jalam and Korah. These are the sons of Esau who were born to him in the land of Canaan.

6   Then Esau took his wives and his sons and his daughters and all his household, and his livestock and all his cattle and all his goods which he had acquired in the land of Canaan, and went to *another* land away from his brother Jacob.

7   For their property had become too great for them to live together, and the land where they sojourned could not sustain them because of their livestock.

8   So Esau lived in the hill country of Seir; Esau is Edom.

9   These then are *the records of* the generations of Esau the father of the Edomites in the hill country of Seir.

10   These are the names of Esau's sons: Eliphaz the son of Esau's wife Adah, Reuel the son of Esau's wife Basemath.

11   The sons of Eliphaz were Teman, Omar, Zepho and Gatam and Kenaz.

12   Timna was a concubine of Esau's son Eliphaz and she bore Amalek to Eliphaz. These are the sons of Esau's wife Adah.

13   These are the sons of Reuel: Nahath and Zerah, Shammah and Mizzah. These were the sons of Esau's wife Basemath.

14   These were the sons of Esau's wife Oholibamah, the daughter of Anah and the granddaughter of Zibeon: she bore to Esau, Jeush and Jalam and Korah.

15   These are the chiefs of the sons of Esau. The sons of Eliphaz, the firstborn of Esau, are chief Teman, chief Omar, chief Zepho, chief Kenaz,

16   chief Korah, chief Gatam, chief Amalek. These are the chiefs descended from Eliphaz in the land of Edom; these are the sons of Adah.

17   These are the sons of Reuel, Esau's son: chief Nahath, chief Zerah, chief Shammah, chief Mizzah. These are the chiefs descended from Reuel in the land of Edom; these are the sons of Esau's wife Basemath.

18 These are the sons of Esau's wife Oholibamah: chief Jeush, chief Jalam, chief Korah. These are the chiefs descended from Esau's wife Oholibamah, the daughter of Anah.

19 These are the sons of Esau (that is, Edom), and these are their chiefs.

20 These are the sons of Seir the Horite, the inhabitants of the land: Lotan and Shobal and Zibeon and Anah,

21 and Dishon and Ezer and Dishan. These are the chiefs descended from the Horites, the sons of Seir in the land of Edom.

22 The sons of Lotan were Hori and Hemam; and Lotan's sister was Timna.

23 These are the sons of Shobal: Alvan and Manahath and Ebal, Shepho and Onam.

24 These are the sons of Zibeon: Aiah and Anah—he is the Anah who found the hot springs in the wilderness when he was pasturing the donkeys of his father Zibeon.

25 These are the children of Anah: Dishon, and Oholibamah, the daughter of Anah.

26 These are the sons of Dishon: Hemdan and Eshban and Ithran and Cheran.

27 These are the sons of Ezer: Bilhan and Zaavan and Akan.

28 These are the sons of Dishan: Uz and Aran.

29 These are the chiefs descended from the Horites: chief Lotan, chief Shobal, chief Zibeon, chief Anah,

30 chief Dishon, chief Ezer, ·chief Dishan. These are the chiefs descended from the Horites, according to their *various* chiefs in the land of Seir.

31 Now these are the kings who reigned in the land of Edom before any king reigned over the sons of Israel.

32 Bela the son of Beor reigned in Edom, and the name of his city was Dinhabah.

33 Then Bela died, and Jobab the son of Zerah of Bozrah became king in his place.

34 Then Jobab died, and Husham of the land of the Temanites became king in his place.

35 Then Husham died, and Hadad the son of Bedad, who defeated Midian in the field of Moab, became king in his place; and the name of his city was Avith.

36 Then Hadad died, and Samlah of Masrekah became king in his place.

37 Then Samlah died, and Shaul of Rehoboth on the *Euphrates* River became king in his place.

38 Then Shaul died, and Baal-hanan the son of Achbor became king in his place.

39 Then Baal-hanan the son of Achbor died, and Hadar became king in his place; and the name of his city was Pau; and his wife's name was Mehetabel, the daughter of Matred, daughter of Mezahab.

40 Now these are the names of the chiefs descended from Esau, according to their families *and* their localities, by their names: chief Timna, chief Alvah, chief Jetheth,

41 chief Oholibamah, chief Elah, chief Pinon,

42 chief Kenaz, chief Teman, chief Mibzar,

43 chief Magdiel, chief Iram. These are the chiefs of Edom (that is, Esau, the father of the Edomites), according to their habitations in the land of their possession.

ACTS 3

1 Now Peter and John were going up to the temple at the ninth *hour*, the hour of prayer.

2   And a man who had been lame from his mother's womb was being carried along, whom they used to set down every day at the gate of the temple which is called Beautiful, in order to beg alms of those who were entering the temple.

3   When he saw Peter and John about to go into the temple, he *began* asking to receive alms.

4   But Peter, along with John, fixed his gaze on him and said, "Look at us!"

5   And he *began* to give them his attention, expecting to receive something from them.

6   But Peter said, "I do not possess silver and gold, but what I do have I give to you: In the name of Jesus Christ the Nazarene—walk!"

7   And seizing him by the right hand, he raised him up; and immediately his feet and his ankles were strengthened.

8   With a leap he stood upright and *began* to walk; and he entered the temple with them, walking and leaping and praising God.

9   And all the people saw him walking and praising God;

10   and they were taking note of him as being the one who used to sit at the Beautiful Gate of the temple to *beg* alms, and they were filled with wonder and amazement at what had happened to him.

11   While he was clinging to Peter and John, all the people ran together to them at the so-called portico of Solomon, full of amazement.

12   But when Peter saw *this*, he replied to the people, "Men of Israel, why are you amazed at this, or why do you gaze at us, as if by our own power or piety we had made him walk?

13   "The God of Abraham, Isaac and Jacob, the God of our fathers, has glorified His servant Jesus, *the one* whom you delivered and disowned in the presence of Pilate, when he had decided to release Him.

14 "But you disowned the Holy and Righteous One and asked for a murderer to be granted to you,

15 but put to death the Prince of life, *the one* whom God raised from the dead, *a fact* to which we are witnesses.

16 "And on the basis of faith in His name, *it is* the name of Jesus which has strengthened this man whom you see and know; and the faith which *comes* through Him has given him this perfect health in the presence of you all.

17 "And now, brethren, I know that you acted in ignorance, just as your rulers did also.

18 "But the things which God announced beforehand by the mouth of all the prophets, that His Christ would suffer, He has thus fulfilled.

19 "Therefore repent and return, so that your sins may be wiped away, in order that times of refreshing may come from the presence of the Lord;

20 and that He may send Jesus, the Christ appointed for you,

21 whom heaven must receive until *the* period of restoration of all things about which God spoke by the mouth of His holy prophets from ancient time.

22 "Moses said, 'THE LORD GOD WILL RAISE UP FOR YOU A PROPHET LIKE ME FROM YOUR BRETHREN; TO HIM YOU SHALL GIVE HEED to everything He says to you.

23 'And it will be that every soul that does not heed that prophet shall be utterly destroyed from among the people.'

24 "And likewise, all the prophets who have spoken, from Samuel and *his* successors onward, also announced these days.

25 "It is you who are the sons of the prophets and of the covenant which God made with your fathers, saying to Abraham, 'AND IN YOUR SEED ALL THE FAMILIES OF THE EARTH SHALL BE BLESSED.'

26 "For you first, God raised up His Servant and sent Him to bless you by turning every one *of you* from your wicked ways."

ACTS 4:1-4

1   As they were speaking to the people, the priests and the captain of the temple *guard* and the Sadducees came up to them,

2   being greatly disturbed because they were teaching the people and proclaiming in Jesus the resurrection from the dead.

3   And they laid hands on them and put them in jail until the next day, for it was already evening.

4   But many of those who had heard the message believed; and the number of the men came to be about five thousand.

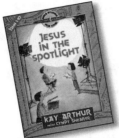

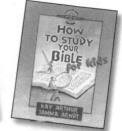

*Kay Arthur
and Cyndy Shearer*
Kids "make" a movie to discover who Jesus is and His impact on their lives. Activities and 15-minute lessons make this study of John 1–10 great for all ages!

ISBN 0-7369-0119-1

Kay Arthur, Janna Arndt, Lisa Guest, and Cyndy Shearer
This book picks up where *Jesus in the Spotlight* leaves off: John 11–16. Kids join a movie team to bring the life of Jesus to the big screen in order to learn key truths about prayer, heaven, and Jesus.

ISBN 0-7369-0144-2

*Kay Arthur
and Janna Arndt*
As "advice columnists," kids delve into the book of James to discover—and learn how to apply—the best answers for a variety of problems.

ISBN 0-7369-0148-5

*Kay Arthur
and Janna Arndt*
This easy-to-use Bible study combines serious commitment to God's Word with illustrations and activities that reinforce biblical truth.

ISBN 0-7369-0362-3

*Kay Arthur and
Janna Arndt*
Focusing on John 17–21, children become "directors" who must discover the details of Jesus' life to make a great movie. They also learn how to get the most out of reading their Bibles.

ISBN 0-7369-0546-4

*Kay Arthur
and Scoti Domeij*
As "reporters," kids investigate Jonah's story and conduct interviews. Using puzzles and activities, these lessons highlight God's loving care and the importance of obedience.

ISBN 0-7369-0203-1

*Kay Arthur
and Janna Arndt*
Kids become archaeologists to uncover how God deals with sin, where different languages and nations came from, and what God's plan is for saving people (Genesis 3–11).

ISBN 0-7369-0374-7

*Kay Arthur
and Janna Arndt*
God's Amazing Creation covers Genesis 1–2—those awesome days when God created the stars, the world, the sea, the animals, and the very first people. Young explorers will go on an archaeological dig to discover truths for themselves!

ISBN 0-7369-0143-4

Kay Arthur and Janna Arndt
The Lord's Prayer is the foundation of this special basic training, and it's not long before the trainees discover the awesome truth that God wants to talk to them as much as they want to talk to Him!

ISBN 0-7369-0666-5

Kay Arthur and Janna Arndt
Readers head out on the rugged Oregon Trail to discover the lessons Abraham learned when he left his home and moved to an unknown land. Kids will face the excitement, fears, and blessings of faith.

ISBN 0-7369-0936-2

Kay Arthur and Janna Arndt
This exciting new book leads the reader on a journey to God's heart using the inductive study method and the wonder of an adventurous spy tale.

ISBN 0-7369-1161-8

Kay Arthur and Janna Arndt
This engaging, high-energy addition to the Discover 4 Yourself series examines the journeys of Isaac, Jacob, and Esau and reveals how God outfits His children with everything they need for life's difficulties, victories, and extreme adventures.

ISBN 0-7369-0937-0

Books in the
New Inductive Study Series

～～～～

Teach Me Your Ways
Genesis, Exodus,
Leviticus, Numbers,
Deuteronomy

**Choosing Victory,
Overcoming Defeat**
Joshua, Judges, Ruth

Desiring God's Own Heart
1 & 2 Samuel,
1 Chronicles

Walking Faithfully with God
1 & 2 Kings, 2 Chronicles

**Overcoming Fear
and Discouragement**
Ezra, Nehemiah, Esther

**Trusting God
in Times of Adversity**
Job

**God's Blueprint for
Bible Prophecy**
Daniel

**Opening the Windows
of Blessings**
Haggai, Zechariah,
Malachi

The Call to Follow Jesus
Luke

**The Holy Spirit
Unleashed in You**
Acts

**Experiencing the Real
Power of Faith**
Romans

**God's Answers for
Relationships and Passions**
1 & 2 Corinthians

**Free from Bondage
God's Way**
Galatians, Ephesians

That I May Know Him
Philippians, Colossians

**Standing Firm in
These Last Days**
1 & 2 Thessalonians

**Walking in Power,
Love, and Discipline**
1 & 2 Timothy, Titus

**Living with Discernment
in the End Times**
1 & 2 Peter, Jude

Behold, Jesus Is Coming!
Revelation